# THE F
# A PRINCIPLED
# FOREIGN POLICY

COMMENTARY AND SELECT SPEECHES FROM
MY FIRST YEAR IN PARLIAMENT

Kidlington Publishing
Vancouver, BC

# GARNETT GENUIS

Printed in Canada

First Printing, 2016

ISBN-13: 978-0-99-533390-1

Kidlington Publishing
1000-355 Burrard Street
Vancouver, BC V6C 2G8

Cover and book design by Saundra Jones, Torch.

*To Blessed Clemens August Graf von Galen, whose courageous opposition to the Nazis saved many lives, including perhaps that of my grandmother, and whose steadfast pursuit of justice is my inspiration.*

**- Nec Laudibus, Nec Timore**

# CONTENTS

# ABOUT THE AUTHOR

Garnett Genuis was first elected in 2015 as the Member of Parliament (MP) for Sherwood Park-Fort Saskatchewan. He is a member of Her Majesty's Loyal Opposition, the Conservative Party of Canada caucus, and he serves as Deputy Critic for Human Rights and Religious Freedom. Genuis has developed a reputation as one of the most outspoken Parliamentarians. According to rankings developed by Maclean's Magazine, he spoke over 100,000 words in the Chamber in his first year as an MP. To put that in context, that is more than all three major party leaders combined, and almost double the total of the next most vocal Conservative MP.

Many of Genuis' speeches focus on international human rights and foreign affairs. He has been extremely active on these issues, drawing attention to various international human rights challenges and calling for a return to Canada's historic principle-based foreign policy. He is also a frequent contributor to the deliberations of the House of Commons Foreign Affairs Committee.

What Maclean's Magazine does not track is the number of words spoken outside the House of Commons. Speaking about foreign affairs and international human rights in university classrooms in India, at rallies on Parliament Hill, and everywhere in between, Genuis has been just as vocal outside the Chamber as inside, if not more.

Genuis grew up in his Edmonton-area constituency, where his interest in international human rights was shaped by the influence of his maternal grandmother, a Holocaust survivor. He studied Public Affairs and Policy Management at Carleton University in Ottawa, and then earned a Masters in Public Policy and Philosophy at the London School of Economics in London, England. Before entering politics as an elected representative, Genuis worked as a 'staffer' in the Prime Minister's Office, a writer and editor at a small online news company, a debate coach at an inner-city school in London, and, most recently, as the vice president of a public opinion research company.

In 2011, Garnett married Rebecca Lobo, a family doctor and daughter of Pakistani Goan immigrants to Canada. Garnett and Rebecca have two young children. In their spare time, they all play highly competitive games of 'Go Fish' and 'Snakes and Ladders.'

Genuis got involved in politics in order to try to make a difference. He contends that the world is rarely changed by those who choose to keep their opinions to themselves.

# INTRODUCTION: THE FIGHT FOR A PRINCIPLED FOREIGN POLICY

## THE POLITICS OF INTEREST AND THE POLITICS OF PRINCIPLE

In politics, whether at the student union, where I started out, or at the United Nations, to which I now pay considerable attention, there is always some balancing of principle and pragmatism. Almost no one seriously suggests that it is possible or desirable to be completely uncompromising. The precise way in which principle and practicality are balanced, then, is at the heart of many of our political conversations.

For some in public life, all decisions are shaped by interests. Those interests could be personal, such as one's own career advancement. They could be political, such as the election of one's party. They could be class or group based, such as the elevation of the relative condition of the poor, or the preservation of privilege for a particular social or ethnic group. They could be national, such as the election of Canada to the Security Council. For those who think in this interest-based way, principles play a secondary role.

As the examples suggest, interests are not necessarily good or bad. They can be selfish or noble; and, their realization can be socially desirable or undesirable. But in any event, the interest-based perspective would emphasize that interests are the only relevant considerations.

Those whose politics have been shaped by a focus on 'interests', especially in the context of foreign policy, are many and are well celebrated – from Machiavelli to Kissinger and beyond. Nobody expressed this elevation of interests over principles better than Kissinger, who once told a congressional committee, "Covert action should not be confused with missionary work."

The people shaping Canada's current foreign policy revolution do not quite have the cut of a Machiavelli or a Kissinger. Yet, the significance of what is happening here should not be under-estimated. This Liberal government knows what it wants; and, it is pursuing clearly-stated foreign policy objectives. Their foreign policy doctrine re-casts Canada's engagement with the world in interest-based terms, instead of principle-based terms.

There is an alternative to the politics of unmoored 'interest'. It is the politics of principle. For me, the politics of principle rests on two inter-related ideas. The first is that there are certain things that have intrinsic value, and that those things must be defended, come hell or high water. 'Intrinsic' value, in this sense, means value that is not dependent on anyone's interest in protecting it. Intrinsic value is not given as an act of someone else's will and is not the result of circumstance. Intrinsic value is the sense that particular kinds of value are embedded in the very nature of a thing. For example, we might say that a person has intrinsic value – meaning that a person is not valued simply based on their usefulness, their experiences, or their social circle, but rather, based on the fact that they are a human being.

The belief in the intrinsic value of people and of certain principles can have many different intellectual origins. It is not the exclusive domain of any particular political or moral philosophy, or of any part of the political spectrum.

Historically, a principle-based concept of intrinsic value has been the basis of almost every claim about human rights. Human rights are rights that accord uniquely to humans on the basis of who and what we are – creatures with a certain inherent worth and dignity. History's great human rights defenders have understood that, while compromises may be made in the pursuit of ends that are of intrinsic value, intrinsic value itself must never be compromised or denied.

And second, the politics of principle holds that our interests, individually, politically, factionally, and nationally, are in the final analysis best advanced by sticking to our principles. In the short term, principles can often seem to get in the way of achieving one's objectives. However, in the long run, there is not much sense in sacrificing principles in order to advance one's interests. Doing so is almost necessarily counterproductive.

Principles may come from a sense of intrinsic value, but they are also useful tools of self-preservation. The identification and public defence of principles, as well as consistent adherence to those principles, increases the likelihood that others will adopt them and treat the proponent of them in the same way. Those who behave solely according to their interests implicitly invite others to do the same. We are all safer in a world where others treat us, individually, politically, and nationally, in a principled way.

This point is well illustrated by a dialogue in "A Man for All Seasons", in which Thomas More tells his son-in-law, "This country is planted thick with laws, from coast to coast, Man's laws, not God's! And if you cut them down, and you're just the man to do it, do you really think you could stand upright in the winds that would blow then? Yes, I'd give the devil benefit of law, for my own safety's sake!" Regardless of where they come from, our common principles of conduct generally leave us all better off.

The politics of principle fundamentally contends that adhering to principle is both intrinsically right and practically useful. The first speech in this book, on the definition of genocide and on the relationship between peace and justice, makes this argument explicitly.

## CHANGE IS AFOOT

In this book, I use commentary and a selection of my speeches, both in the Canadian House of Commons and outside it, to draw attention to the transformation that is underway in Canadian foreign policy.

The previous Conservative government, imperfectly but sincerely, applied a principle-based lens to foreign policy decisions. This approach periodically won acclaim across the political spectrum, finding adherents even within the Liberal Party. Yet, to some Canadian Liberals, this approach was not only wrong-headed, it was entirely unintelligible. To them, foreign policy is by nature about interests. Operating on their reading of interests, they simply could not understand some of the strong positions we took.

Because of their assumption that everything is ultimately rooted in interests, Liberals often concluded that the 'principled' positions which the Conservative government took were really about a different kind of interest – partisan interest. To these cynics, everything was always about currying favour with diaspora communities: Support for Israel was about the Jewish vote, meeting with the Dalai Lama was about the Tibetan vote, and the creation of the Office of Religious Freedom was about outreach to target communities facing religious persecution.

This particular criticism is addressed parenthetically in this book's second speech, "In Defense of the Office of Religious Freedom". Notably, those who insist on viewing principled foreign policy decisions through a political lens never account for the fact that, while these decisions had positive political implications in certain communities, they also had significant potential negative political implications in others. There is no concentration of Tibetans voters in any constituency that is plausibly winnable for the Conservative Party, for example, and Jewish voters make up a very small percentage of the population compared to other communities.

The Liberal Party in opposition, while often seeming perplexed by the Conservative approach to foreign policy, was at a loss to present a compelling alternative. They therefore supported, or at least went along with, many (though not all) of the principled foreign policy positions taken. They rarely directly criticized Conservative support for Israel; they were much more measured in their desire for increased engagement with Iran; they explicitly supported the implementation of special sanctions against Russian human rights abusers (known as "Magnitsky Sanctions"); and they did not oppose the creation of the Office of Religious Freedom. While many Liberals seem to have wanted a different kind of foreign policy, they were rarely active in their criticism of particular measures. A foreign policy based on the pursuit of interests, they seemed to realize, is as hard to sell to the general public as it is easy to implement.

Once in power, the Liberals initiated a significant shift in foreign policy. It's difficult for me, from the opposition benches, to speculate about whether there was an actual 'shift' in Liberal thinking behind the policy change, or whether this was a planned pivot all along. Regardless, there has been an unmistakable shift away from both the approach taken by the previous Conservative government and that of the Liberals in opposition.

Shortly after his appointment as foreign minister, Stephane Dion was, according to the media outlet iPolitics, musing about Canada returning to an "honest broker" role in the Middle East. This term is obviously ambiguous. However, in this context, it is generally understood to mean that a country is declining to 'take sides' in favour of freedom and democracy – and is instead taking a more neutral position somewhere in between that of free democracies on the one hand, and the rest of the world on the other.

This government makes no attempt to hide its intentions to strengthen relations with Iran, even highlighting the possible economic benefits that could come with stronger ties. When speaking about business opportunities in Iran, a minister went so far as to highlight opportunities associated with a growing Iranian demand for civilian aircraft. Given the Iranian pursuit of advanced missile technology, there is something eerie about highlighting aerospace opportunities in Iran.

Breaking a pre-election commitment, the Liberal government appears to no longer support special sanctions for Russian human rights abusers – the "Magnitsky Sanctions" referred to above. The Prime Minister no longer intends to call out Vladimir Putin for invading Ukraine, even though he said he would during the election campaign. The government also shut down the Office of Religious Freedom, ostensibly so as to protect human rights in some other way. Perhaps most disappointingly, on June 14th, 2016, government MPs overwhelmingly opposed a Conservative motion to label the atrocities of Daesh/ISIS against certain religious minorities as genocide – even though the Parliaments of the European Union and the United Kingdom, as well as the American Congress and Administration adopted unanimous or nearly-unanimous resolutions to that affect.

In any revolution, there is some degree of give and take. Minister Dion did concede some ground on the genocide issue after a UN body started using the word. The Office of Religious Freedom was, after much delay and substantial pressure, replaced with a still largely undefined new 'Office of Human Rights, Freedom, and Inclusion.' Notably, the Office of Religious Freedom was led by an Ambassador, while the new office will simply be led by a director. Without an Ambassador, this new office is unlikely to have anywhere near the prominence or profile that that previous office did. In any event, the broad trend is unmistakable – a movement from clear stands on human rights and intrinsic human dignity, to a more quiet and inoffensive policy - the movement from 'principles' to 'interests'.

## EXPLAINING THE SHIFT

Having explained this foreign policy shift in terms of specific policy areas, it is also important to highlight two key events which explain this foreign policy shift in broader terms. There were two particularly revealing moments in the first months of this government which set the stage for this shift. The first of these was the government's decision to explicitly and publically lay out its plan to actively campaign for a seat on the UN Security Council. The second was a speech Minister Dion gave at the University of Ottawa in which he attempted to distance himself from the term "honest broker", while also rejecting the principle-based approach (what he called a 'conviction'-based approach) of the previous government.

Conservatives have a range of views on the United Nations. Most of us would regard it as an important and useful institution with some serious flaws. It is an institution that requires our active engagement; however, we should not unthinkingly submit to its mechanisms or protocols, especially in cases where they do not accord with our principles.

Many Canadian Liberals would probably assent to that broad outline as well. But there is no doubt that the UN has a different place in Liberal mythology. Liberals generally do not regard the UN as just another potentially useful international institution. To the extent that they believe in this category, it sometimes seems that they see the UN itself as verging on an 'intrinsic good'.

The previous Conservative government sought a seat on the UN Security Council, and did not succeed. This was a minor failure in the minds of many Conservatives; a disappointment, but not that big a deal. Conservatives accounted for this by suggesting that it was a response to our principled foreign policy. We took pride in the fact that we would not sacrifice our principles to curry favour at the UN - while still wishing it would have been possible for things to go differently. This sense that we lost partly because of our principles has validity to it. However, our defeat probably also had a lot to do with the bloc-oriented behaviour of certain groups of countries, working to get one of their cohorts onto the Security Council instead. In any event, this was unfortunate, but largely unavoidable – or at least, not avoidable at an acceptable cost.

For Liberals, however, our defeat in the Security Council election was a watershed moment, a disaster, and a repudiation of the entire foreign policy approach of the Harper government. Without directly criticizing most of the specific positions the previous government took, Liberals firmly contended that our foreign policy was, in general, a failure. Given their unshakeable faith in the UN process, this defeat was proof positive of how bad things allegedly were.

So upon taking power, it was an immediate priority for the new Liberal government to chart a course to get Canada onto the Security Council again. On March 16th, 2016, the Prime Minister personally announced that Canada would be seeking a seat on the council, with our prospective term starting in 2021. The government had previously announced its intent to seek the seat, without announcing a specific timeline. Everything about the rollout of this, especially the multiple announcements by the Prime Minister, was clearly designed to underscore how important this was to the government.

Here's what I had to say about this announcement, in an interview with the CBC: "It's worth seeking the seat, there's no harm in seeking a seat ... but the question will be, 'At what cost?' ... Our approach on foreign policy was to engage with the United Nations, but to do it in a way that was principled... not to compromise on things like human rights and support for Israel, support for religious and ethnic minorities, and what we're already seeing from this government, frankly, is a step back from that principled foreign policy."

In other words, there's no harm, and some value, in Canada seeking this seat; but, it is not worth compromising our principles. Fundamentally, nothing is worth compromising our principles. But furthermore, it is not in our long-term interest to cozy up to everyone with a vote at the UN. A variety of different political dynamics, especially the increasing European inclination to bloc-vote for their own, will make winning a seat on the Security Council quite difficult. Winning a seat seems to be possible only by fully re-orienting key aspects of our diplomacy, trade policy, and development assistance policy towards winning over swing voters. This is the politics of 'interest' at its finest – the sacrifice of anything in the pursuit of particular chosen objectives.

In the first "Outside the Chamber" speech in this book, I discuss directly one possible result of this focus on the UN bid: the elimination of the Office of Religious Freedom. Since religious and ethnic minorities do not have a vote at the UN, they are not a priority. States vote, so states are the priority.

I mentioned two defining moments which marked our foreign policy shift. The first was the UN announcement. The second was a speech given by Minister Dion, in which he set out the defining philosophy of his foreign policy. Politicians rarely bother to outline in thoughtful and detailed terms the nature of their motivating philosophy, and I commend Dion for doing so in this case. This speech, though a relatively academic one, was widely covered – perhaps showing that, even in the age of Twitter and Buzzfeed, there is an appetite for serious and thoughtful discussion of policy questions. Here is what the Minister had to say:

> "The guiding principle that I will follow in fulfilling this mandate is something I call responsible conviction. Let me explain what I mean by that.
>
> "I refer you to the traditional distinction that Max Weber made between the ethics of conviction and the ethics of responsibility. Weber contrasted behaviour that remains true to one's convictions, regardless of what happens (ethics of conviction), and behaviour that takes the consequences of one's actions into consideration (ethics of responsibility). In isolation, the ethics of conviction of course lead to pure action, defending a principle or a cause, while ignoring the consequences. Pacifists who recommend unilateral disarmament in the face of the enemy are inspired by the ethics of conviction: they advocate non-violence at all times.
>
> "Such behaviour is rejected from the point of view of

the ethics of responsibility. For example, although Gandhi's pacifism delivered results in the face of a British democracy that doubted the legitimacy of its empire, it obviously would have had disastrous results in the face of Hitler's army.

"Max Weber did not claim that those who support the ethics of responsibility lack conviction. But since this is how he is often misinterpreted, I prefer to go beyond his rigid distinction to create a more syncretic concept – the ethics of 'responsible conviction.' This formulation means that my values and convictions include the sense of responsibility. Not considering the consequences of my words and actions on others would be contrary to my convictions. I feel I am responsible for the consequences of my actions."

He continues later in the speech, "Canadian foreign policy has lacked responsible conviction in recent years. It must be principled, but less dogmatic and more focused on delivering results. Responsible conviction must not be confused with some sort of moral relativism. Since the classic concept of the honest broker is now too often confused with moral relativism or the lack of strong convictions, I prefer to say that Canada must be a fair-minded and determined peace builder."

This speech wades deeply into the question of principle versus pragmatism. Despite the efforts to move away from explicit moral relativism, it clearly marked an intention to further elevate the relative position of 'pragmatism' in the balance.

Some critics pointed out that this exercise in providing philosophical definition to the government approach did not go that far at all towards providing actual clarity. What does an ethic of 'responsible conviction' lead us to do when it comes to any number of specific and thorny policy questions? The answer to that probably depends on other philosophical commitments as well as individual assessments of the likely consequences of particular courses of action. In practise, the ambiguity of this lens gives the minister a mechanism to justify almost anything.

Furthermore, although academic in style, Dion's speech had all the trappings of a standard political "all of the above" speech. Politicians frequently fail to recognize the reality of hard choices. When asked if they would prioritize human rights or international trade, the economy or the environment, national security or civil liberties, they often want to say "we can do both". This is often partially true, but also sometimes an evasion. Governing is ultimately about making choices, and sometimes about choosing between competing values. Any politician who always insists that they can have their cake and eat it too is probably not being forthright. Dion's doctrine of 'responsible conviction' is essentially a formalization of having your cake and eating it too. As I said at the beginning, nobody seriously disagrees with the need to consider both principles and pragmatism, but actually outlining a coherent foreign policy involves going a little further than pointing that out.

Still, to the extent that it is specific, Dion's 'responsible conviction' does not seem to accept that there are certain principles of foreign policy which are inviolable. On this point, I firmly disagree with Dion. For the reasons of intrinsic value and long-term consequentialism described above, there are certain things we should never do, or tolerate, or ignore – even if we think our interests, however defined, are best served by violating those principles.

Though not announced clearly during the 2015 election campaign, the government is fundamentally re-orienting our foreign policy. I believe that this re-orientation is wrong, and is at odds with Canadian values.

## SOME PRACTICAL NOTES

The speeches selected for this book focus around key arguments for a principle-based response to the turmoil the world currently faces. The speeches are divided into three sections –

speeches given in the House of Commons on foreign policy and human rights, speeches given outside of it on these same topics, and a couple speeches from the chamber on different but related topics.

The speeches from inside the chamber contain virtually identical text to that which appears in Hansard (the official Parliamentary record). I did, however, correct a few small but important transcription errors. In one case, former Pakistani politician Shahbaz Bhatti appears in Hansard as "Chavez Bhatti". In another, the Hansard text refers to "duel citizens" – who, one might suppose, are citizens who engage regularly in one-on-one combat. My speech intended, however, to refer to "dual citizens," and I have made the correction here.

Each speech is preceded by a brief introduction in which I explain the context. These sections sometimes describe relevant 'quirks' of the Parliamentary process, although in a couple places I have used notes in the middle of the text instead. A number of the speeches are from what we call "Opposition Days." These are days in the Parliamentary calendar which are allotted to opposition parties to put forward motions on issues important to them. These motions are debated for the duration of the allotted day, and then voted on, either that evening or a few days later. Most of the Parliamentary calendar is consumed by debate on bills put forward by the government, so these Opposition Days provide important opportunities for opposition parties to ensure some discussion of what they consider important.

While some people would refer to all Members of Parliament as part of the "government," this is not technically correct. The government consists of the Prime Minister, Ministers, perhaps Parliamentary Secretaries, public servants, and sometimes more informally the MPs who belong to the governing party.

I hope, after reading all or parts of this book, that you will join me in seeking to put pressure on the government to reverse their foreign policy shift. In addition to being compiled here, the speeches given in the chamber are also accessible online, in easily shareable formats.

I would welcome and appreciate your direct feedback, your thoughtful objections, and your willingness to share elements of your own experience in these areas. I invite you to contact me directly or through my office.

*-Garnett Genuis*

# PART 1
# IN THE CHAMBER

# THE RELATIONSHIP BETWEEN PEACE AND JUSTICE: DEFINING GENOCIDE

JUNE 9th, 2016

*I have placed the speeches in each section of this book in roughly reverse chronological order; and, it is quite appropriate that this one happens to come first. In this speech I lay out some key aspects and principles of my approach to foreign policy. This speech was given as part of the debate about whether or not to identify as 'genocide' the atrocities being committed against Yazidis, Assyrian Christians, and other religious minorities in Syria and Iraq. This motion was opposed by the government.*

On the relationship between peace and justice, there is a theoretical tension between these two. The pursuit of peace may on certain readings in certain situations require us to let go of things we would rather address, to allow to pass by things which we would rather confront but the confrontation of which would lead to a loss of peace.

On the other hand, the pursuit of justice may put us in conflict with others, with the purveyors of injustice and with those who, while desiring justice of a certain kind, have a different conception of justice than we do. When peace is valued over justice, we are inclined to leave injustice unaddressed. When justice is valued over peace, we risk regular conflict even between those with good intentions on the basis of rival conceptions of justice.

I do not just mean military conflict in the context of loss of peace but also conflict as in a disruption of favour and goodwill, and perhaps conflict in terms of being opposed in our ambitions. The pursuit of justice always upsets the tranquillity of life, in this context, the relative potential tranquillity of Canadian international diplomatic relations.

During our previous Conservative government we regularly put the pursuit of justice ahead of tranquillity in international relations. We stood for what was and is right. We stood for the rights of persecuted religious, ethnic, and linguistic minorities. We stood for the right of self-determination for any peaceful community. We stood for the right of the Jewish people to a safe and secure homeland. We stood for the right of the Russian people to know that human rights abusers from their country will not be able to travel to and invest in the west. We stood for the rights of Chinese Uighurs, Afghani Sikhs, Crimean Tatars, and yes, Yazidis, Christians, Kurds, Turkmen, Shia Muslims, and other groups in the path of Daesh.

We were willing to stand up and upset our tranquillity in the process. We believed that a country in pursuit of justice might have to pay a price for its stand, but that it was right that we be prepared to pay that price.

This government has a fundamentally different approach when it comes to foreign affairs. While we believed and believe deeply in the pursuit of justice, this government values peace, values tranquillity, over justice. The Liberals are not prepared to speak clearly about international human rights. They are downgrading our capacities in this respect and they are refusing to speak the truth about injustice. In this particular case, they are refusing to call a genocide what it is.

Now many of my colleagues have already spoken eloquently about why using the term genocide is not only justified, but is necessary in the case of Daesh actions towards Yazidis and Christians in Syria and Iraq.

The UN Convention on the Prevention and Punishment of the Crime of Genocide defines genocide as:

"...any of the following acts committed with intent to destroy, in whole or in part, a national, ethnical, racial or religious group, as such:

(a) Killing members of the group;

(b) Causing serious bodily or mental harm to members of the group;

(c) Deliberately inflicting on the group conditions of life calculated to bring about its physical destruction in whole or in part;

(d) Imposing measures intended to prevent births within the group;

(e) Forcibly transferring children of the group to another group."

Any one of these conditions is a sufficient basis to qualify as genocide, but there is clear, documented evidence that Daesh has engaged in all five of these things. That is why the American administration, the American Congress, the British Parliament, and the European Parliament have all recognized this as a genocide. Are we to seriously believe that our Minister of Foreign Affairs is wiser or happens to know something these august bodies do not?

The best that the Liberals can come up with in opposition to this is to assert that our membership in the International Criminal Court in some way prevents us from calling this a genocide.

The only thing worse than using legalese to cover moral cowardice is using bad, ill-informed, made-up legalese to cover moral cowardice. Every single EU country is a member of the ICC. They have all recognized the genocide through a motion very similar to this. The parliamentary secretary said it was just a motion in the European context. This is a motion as well, and our recognition of genocide should not be and need not be held up by a Security Council veto.

These arguments are obviously not the point. The evidence is clear and international law is clear with respect to what genocide is. We know it is clear, they know it is clear, and we know that they know it is clear. However, they still will not use the word "genocide", quite obviously because there is a certain safety, a certain comfort, a certain tranquillity, in resisting taking a stand and holding back on the call for justice; because using the word "genocide" upsets our peace. It is a disruptive word because it crystalizes and clarifies the truly evil nature of Daesh and our moral and legal obligation to respond in a serious way. The government prefers similar but sufficiently unclear language in this, so as to appear to be roughly on the same page but not to upset the Liberals' desired foreign-policy focus of peace and tranquillity as opposed to the pursuit of justice.

Why is it necessary to speak the truth in this case? Why is it necessary to call a genocide a genocide? Why do we take the denial of genocides, historic or present, so seriously? I have spoken before in the House about my grandmother's story. My grandmother was a Holocaust survivor, one of millions of European Jews who suffered in some way because of Hitler's efforts to exterminate them.

On August 22, 1939, about a week before the invasion of Poland, Hitler gave what has come to be known as the Obersalzberg speech to his military commanders, in which he laid out his genocidal intent, in this case toward the Polish people. For our understanding of history, of how and why genocides happen, it is important to know what he said:

"...our war aim does not consist of reaching certain lines, but in the physical destruction of the enemy. Accordingly, I have placed my death-head formations in readiness...with orders to them to send to death mercilessly and without compassion, men, women, and children of Polish derivation and language. Only thus shall we gain the living space...we need. Who, after all, speaks today of the annihilation of the Armenians?"

In this seminal address to his commanders, it was important for Hitler to reflect on the absence of international recognition or regard for the Armenian genocide. This was not the first time that

Hitler invoked a comparison between the Armenian genocide and his intended plans. He inferred from the experience of the Armenians that nobody would care if he killed the Jews.

When we stand in the House to remember and recognize the Holocaust, the Armenian genocide, the Holodomor, and other such events, we are not just engaging in a collective exercise in the study of history. We are remembering because reminding ourselves of the reality of past evil, ensuring that violence against the innocent is condemned over and over again in the strongest possible terms, is a way of ensuring that we finally learn the lessons of history. As much as it upsets our tranquillity from time to time to call out evil, in the past or the present, it must be done. What good is remembering the past if we only pay attention to genocides that happened decades ago? The failure to confront evil in the present is precisely what leads tyrants in the future to conclude that their contemporaries will not care either. To call out evil, to speak the truth about international human rights, to do so in a way that is clear and unambiguous may cost us friends and goodwill; it may cost us more still. However, it is the only thing that prevents would-be tyrants of this world from believing that they will get away with it.

On the relationship between peace and justice, there is, yes, a theoretical tension between the two, but there is also an essential unity between the two. Those who violate the basic rights and dignity of their own people invariably become a menace to their neighbours and the entire community of civilized nations, as Daesh has already become. It is not in the nature of tyrants to, on the one hand, overthrow the domestic rule of law and then to respect international law, on the other. It is a certainty that those who are a menace to justice in their own land will be a menace to peace, if not right away then eventually. Even on consequential grounds, it makes sense to stand up for justice in the first instance, but more important, we cannot call ourselves a just society if we refuse to speak clearly about justice on the international stage.

That is justice in the pursuit of peace, and justice that is disruptive to peace, because the 19 Yazidi girls who were burned alive in a cage this week are every bit as human as the members here or my daughter or their daughters. If members would call it a genocide for themselves or their people group, then they should do it for someone else's.

# IN DEFENCE OF THE OFFICE
# OF RELIGIOUS FREEDOM

MARCH 21st, 2016

*I spent a significant amount of time during my first year in Parliament fighting for the renewal, and then for the restoration, of the Office of Religious Freedom. The Office was set to expire (and did) on the 31st of March, 2016. On March 21st, ten days before the metaphorical axe fell, I was given an opportunity to propose and defend an Opposition Day motion, calling for the renewal of the Office of Religious Freedom. Going into the debate that morning, I believed that there was a genuine chance that this motion would receive government support. I therefore crafted arguments that I hoped would be convincing to government members. I reference my own family history in many different speeches; however, this was an opportunity to draw on the history of my wife's family, every bit as fascinating and revealing as my own. This was my first twenty minute speech in the House, the culmination of months and months of work, and a chance to pay tribute to my wife's heritage. The time gave me an opportunity both to tell stories and to make clear, distinct arguments.*

Mr. Speaker, on May 16, 1919, Molly Pinto was born in Karachi, Pakistan, then part of greater India. Her family was originally from Goa, a Portuguese colony on the west coast of India, which had and continues to have a large Catholic population. She grew up in a Goan Catholic colony in Karachi. She remembered a very happy childhood, one populated by children and then young adults from all different ethnic and religious communities: Goan, as well as indigenous Pakistani Christians, Muslims, Hindus, Sikhs, Jews, etc. Various languages were spoken: English; Konkani, the Goan language; Urdu; Hindi; etc. She recalls how people from different communities shared meaningful friendships. They would bring sweets to their Muslim neighbours at Christmastime, and their neighbours would bring them sweets for Eid.

Molly Pinto is my wife's grandmother, and the Pakistan that she grew up in looked a lot like how Canada looks today. Those on the left and on the right who are willing to casually label religious intolerance as part of the culture or religion in Pakistan do not know their history. Countries like Pakistan had a rich tradition of multicultural, multilingual, multi-faith co-operation long before Canada even existed, and that tradition continues in the living memory of many who are still with us today. I am sure that some members of the House remember that history from their own experience, and hope and pray for a return to it.

Molly remembers how increasing tensions emerged during partition, when India and Pakistan achieved their independence and separated from each other. Her perception was that when people who had been pushed out of other places in present-day India came to Pakistan, often after seeing or experiencing violence at home, they brought a level of suspicion and tension that felt alien in what had previously been an idyllic setting.

Still, Mohammad Ali Jinnah, the founder of Pakistan, was very clear about the need to continue Pakistan's pluralistic traditions after independence. Like Molly, Jinnah was born in Karachi. His family were Gujarati Shia Muslims, and as a Shia, Jinnah was in many senses part of a religious minority as well. He also attended Christian schools.

Jinnah had a vision for Pakistan that made the protection of minorities central to its success. Pakistan adopted a flag which clearly demonstrated his vision, a green section to represent the Muslim majority, and a white stripe for the minority communities.

Here is what Muhammad Ali Jinnah said in an address to the constituent assembly of Pakistan in 1947:

"You are free; you are free to go to your temples, you are free to go to your mosques or to any other place or worship in this State of Pakistan. You may belong to any religion or caste or creed that has nothing to do with the business of the State. [...] We are starting in the days where there is no discrimination, no distinction between one community and another, no discrimination between one caste or creed and another. We are starting with this fundamental principle that we are all citizens and equal citizens of one State."

On September 9, 1968, Clement Shahbaz Bhatti was born in Lahore, Pakistan. He would go on to become the country's first federal minister for minority affairs. In 1979, when Shahbaz was 11 years old, the Soviet Union invaded Afghanistan. This event would have a consequential impact on world affairs, in Pakistan, and in the life of Shahbaz Bhatti .

Western aid, and aid from other Muslim countries, was funnelled through Pakistan to support the mujahedeen in its jihad against the Soviet Union. The mujahedeen defeated the Soviets, but Pakistan paid a heavy price for its involvement because of the significant injection of extreme and intolerant ideas that came with the mujahedeen and subsequent rise of the Taliban. The rise of extremism in Iran, as well, had a negative effect on Pakistani pluralism.

Importantly, none of these developments in the Muslim world were inevitable. They reflected the push and pull of history, perhaps some policy mistakes, perhaps some policy decisions which were necessary in their time but that had unintended consequences. Either way, the evident decline of pluralism in Pakistan was not inevitable, and it is not irreversible.

Shahbaz Bhatti knew that. As federal minister for minorities in Pakistan, he visited Canada. He came here in February 2011, the month before his assassination. He met with the former prime minister as well as other ministers. He knew then how vulnerable he was. His visit followed on the heels of the assassination of Governor Salmaan Taseer, a Pakistani Muslim who, like Shahbaz, was an outspoken critic of Pakistan's blasphemy laws used to target religious minorities.

It was Shabazz's legacy and the advocacy work of his family here in Canada which led the previous Conservative government to act to create the Office of Religious Freedom. It was not some theoretical political statement about abstract rights, but an office that would and has made a real difference for people in Pakistan and all around the world.

What is the Office of Religious Freedom? The Office of Religious Freedom was established as a division of foreign affairs, now Global Affairs Canada, in the last Parliament. Incidentally, the creation of this office was announced inside a mosque. The office has an annual budget of $5 million, which is a modest sum in the scheme of things. This is 1/180th of the cost of the government's recent changes to public sector sick leave, and it is well underneath the cost of renovating 24 Sussex Drive.

This office does three main things. First, it provides training to the public service. This training is crucial to help our public servants understand underlying religious tensions and how to advance human rights and Canada's interests in the context of these dynamics.

U.S. Secretary of State John Kerry has said, "...if I went back to college today, I think I would probably major in comparative religion, because that's how integrated it is in everything that we are working on and deciding and thinking about in life today."

Helping Canada's foreign policy be informed by an understanding of religious tensions is critical in the current environment.

Second, this office does direct advocacy, speaking out about and bringing attention to the plight of persecuted religious minorities.

Third, this office funds direct on-the-ground projects with local partners in countries like Pakistan, projects which advance religious freedom. That is in fact where most of the budget goes.

This office has had considerable success. However, members do not have to take my word for it. Here is what the Parliamentary Secretary to the Minister of Foreign Affairs, Consular Affairs, the member for Mississauga Centre, had to say recently about the work of the office in Ukraine:

"As a part of broader efforts to cultivate long-term stability, tolerance, and respect for human rights, including freedom of religion or belief, Global Affairs Canada, through the Office of Religious Freedom, is supporting two projects in Ukraine to promote interfaith dialogue and to strengthen the capacity of local authorities to respond to hate crimes.

As the hon. member is aware, the Office of Religious Freedom has advocated on behalf of religious communities under threat, opposed religious hatred and intolerance, and promoted pluralism and respect for diversity abroad."

The quote continues:

"As the Minister of Foreign Affairs has already stated repeatedly, we are grateful for Dr. Andrew Bennett's service as the head of the Office of Religious Freedom and for his ingenuity, sensitivity, and competency over the past three years."

That is clearly very high praise for this office from the member for Mississauga Centre.

Here is what the Parliamentary Secretary to the Minister of Foreign Affairs, the member for West Vancouver—Sunshine Coast—Sea to Sky Country, had to say recently about the work of the office in Nigeria:

"In its efforts to combat Boko Haram's history of inter-communal violence in the region, Canada, through the Office of Religious Freedom, supported a two-year project to promote interfaith dialogue and conflict mediation in Plateau State, Nigeria. We are well aware of the good work it has done. The project successfully developed a community-based mechanism to help defuse tensions between different religious and ethnic groups, and has been used by the Nigerian government on various occasions, including in response to attacks and bombings in Jos and in the lead up to Nigeria's elections in March 2015. While this phase of the project concluded in January 2015, our government is pleased that Canada has been able to continue to support this model for inter-communal dialogue in neighbouring conflict-affected regions in Nigeria...."

Listening to those eloquent words from Liberal members, one might wonder who could possibly be opposed to this office. Who could possibly oppose this clearly good and necessary work? Given the evidence and given this good work, one might be inclined to think it would be obvious that this office should be renewed. I believe it is obvious. However, there have been critics, and it is important to take this opportunity to respond to some of the arguments that the critics have made.

There are some who seem to have something of an allergy to any office of government which uses the word "religion". They react negatively to any reference to religion in the context of government action. Let us be very clear about this. This office is not about promoting religion. It is about promoting religious freedom. These are two fundamentally different things.

Western democratic governments are not in the business of promoting religion, but all governments have to be in the business of protecting freedom, including freedom of religion. Notably, those who ask for state non-interference in religion are themselves expressing support for religious freedom.

Religious freedom includes atheists. It includes the right not to believe. In fact, atheists have direct representation on the Office of Religious Freedom's external advisory committee. The right to believe as a non-believer is frankly one of the most threatened expressions of religious freedom in the world today. Canada's Office of Religious Freedom advocates for atheists in countries like Bangladesh, where they are particularly vulnerable.

Freedom of religion is not a strictly religious idea. It is recognized in article 18 of the UN charter. It states:

"Everyone has the right to freedom of thought, conscience and religion; this right includes freedom to change his religion or belief, and freedom, either alone or in community with others and in public or private, to manifest his religion or belief in teaching, practice, worship and observance."

If not about religion as such, what is freedom of religion all about?

The UN charter has it right. Freedom of religion is fundamentally about freedom of thought, the freedom for people to think about their fundamental purpose, their place in the universe, and then to act that out how they see fit. This freedom of thought is clearly essential to the human experience. Freedom of religion is about so much more than the phenomenological elements of religion. It is in fact something entirely different in kind. Again, the office exists to promote religious freedom, the kind of freedom of thought identified in the UN charter. It is not about promoting religion.

A second objection we have heard is from those who say that human rights are universal, interdependent, and indivisible, and therefore they do not see a need for a separate office of religious freedom. Of course, we can all agree that rights are interdependent and indivisible. However, we are also well served by centres of excellence within government and within the department of Global Affairs, which focus on specific areas.

To name another example, we have a department for the status of women. Certainly, human rights are universal, interdependent, and indivisible, but we still have, and we should have, a department that focuses specifically on the status of women.

Why is it important that we have these types of centres of excellence? Because to have all types of rights lumped together risks a situation in which no one is focused upon individual specific areas of rights and rights violations. Without specific centres of excellence, individual areas that need attention could risk getting lost in one murky interdependent and indivisible soup.

Interdependence and indivisibility have never before been used as arguments against some degree of specialization. The natural sciences are interdependent and indivisible, yet we are still well served by having those who specialize in chemistry, biology, physics, and in subparts of each.

A third objection we have heard is from those who say that this is merely a political ploy, that the creation of the office was designed for so-called pandering to ethnocultural diaspora communities in Canada. A writer for iPolitics said this in 2013:

"Diaspora politics can become a double-edged sword if left in the hands of politicians. As evidence, look no further than the new Office of Religious Freedom — a policy outcome one might expect when parties curry favour with particular ethnic constituencies."

There was something very dark about these kinds of arguments. So-called ethnic constituencies have as much right to expect that their priorities are reflected in government policy as anyone else. It is true that new Canadians, who are more likely to have ongoing personal and familial connections to those facing religious persecution in other countries, tend to be particularly supportive of this office. However, to describe policies that reflect the priorities of new Canadians as pandering is unnecessarily pejorative and it is a unique kind of pejorative tone often used to denigrate policies that are important to new Canadians.

It is certainly also true that this policy is not just important to new Canadians. Members of diaspora communities, which have been in Canada for generations, and really all Canadians, can see the value of the work that is being done here.

A fourth objection we have heard is from those who suggested the office is supposedly just about Christians and the preferencing of Christian concerns in international affairs. Of note should be the fact that this objection and the previous objection are in fact mutually exclusive and yet are often made simultaneously by the same people. The office could not possibly be both about focusing on Christians and also aimed at new ethnocultural communities. However, it would be evident to anyone who looks at the list of projects the office supports that it works with and for a wide range of different communities.

For example, a recent project gave $290,000 to the Aga Khan Foundation for development and distribution of children's books that promoted pluralism among school-aged children in Bangladesh. Working through a Muslim organization, this project also particularly is important to the atheist community, which faces growing persecution in Bangladesh. Non-Christian groups, in fact, Sikh, Jewish and Muslim leaders in Canada have taken the lead on calling for the renewal of this office. Earlier this year, representatives from these three communities sent a joint letter to the Minister of Foreign Affairs pleading with him to do the right thing and to renew this office.

A vast range of communities are represented on the office's external advisory committee. Muslims, Jews, Sikhs, Buddhists, Christians and, yes, atheists are represented on the external advisory committee as well.

With respect to this objection, it is important to note that this office does provide some support to some Christians. Christians are indisputably one of the most persecuted religious communities anywhere in the world. Long-standing Christian communities, which have existed in the Middle East since almost the time of Christ and since long before Christianity spread to western Europe, or certainly North America, are under intense pressure, which includes, in various cases, systematic discrimination, growing cultural bias, regular violence, and even attempts at total extermination. These people happen to share a faith with western colonizers, but these indigenous Christian communities bear no responsibility whatsoever for colonization. They have as much right to live in peace and security as anyone else.

When I talked to other non-Christian faith groups, strikingly they often raised the increasingly desperate plight of Christians as a matter of significant concern. CIJA, the Centre for Israel and Jewish Affairs, for example, has been vocal in support of the plight of persecuted Christians, and we should listen to what it has to say in this respect. This office does not focus uniquely on Christians but does not ignore them either.

A fifth and final objection that I hear to the Office of Religious Freedom is that its work is in some way colonialist. A recent commentary piece in the Toronto Star said:

"The international promotion of religious freedom by Western states risks repeating 'civilizing' colonial missions, imposing fixed standards without sensitivity to cultural and historical specificities..."

Those who suggest that the good work this office is doing to advance religious freedom is somehow about advancing narrowly western values clearly do not understand the work of this office or the context in which it operates. This office does not seek to dictate to other countries. It works with and provides vital support for programs on the ground. It works with local leaders and leverages local knowledge. That is why it has earned such high praise from diaspora communities and others with whom it directly works.

This is not about western values but about universal human values laid out very clearly in article 18 of the Universal Declaration of Human Rights. Those who object to the promotion of religious freedom on the grounds that it is a "western" value are often the same people who have the same objections to efforts to advance gender equality, democracy, and other principles of human society, which have long been recognized as universal.

Because of my family's connection to Pakistan, I can speak best to our work in that country. Very clearly we are not interested in promoting some western construction of what Pakistan should be. We want to see the restoration of the pluralistic Pakistan that my wife's grandmother Molly grew up in. This was her reality. This was Mohammad Ali Jinnah's vision, and this was Shahbaz Bhatti's dream: the restoration of Pakistan's historic traditions, not the imposition of western ones.

When it comes to this office, the government has refused to give a clear answer. However, with 10 days to go until the current mandate runs out, it is high time it communicates its decision, and this motion is necessary to give people working in this area the clarity they need. Most important, people who rely on this office are waiting for an answer.

If the government recognizes the good work of this office, will it simply say yes so the work can continue uninterrupted? If it is determined to kill this office, could it at least explain why, could it at least give us some kind of a reason?

Two weeks ago, I attended a commemoration held in Toronto to honour Shabaz Bhatti. There I met Rimsha Masih, a Christian teenager who was accused of blasphemy in Pakistan and only found safety after being spirited away to Canada. I think of my wife's grandmother's reality as a child in pluralistic Pakistan. I think now of Rimsha's reality with the challenges facing Pakistan. This is why this work and this motion matter so much. For one-quarter of the cost of the recent member's office budget increase, this office is saving lives and giving hope to people like her. Therefore, I urge members to reflect on the good work this office is doing and to please support this motion.

# SUPPORTING ISRAEL AND OPPOSING ANTI-SEMITISM

### FEBRUARY 18th, 2016

*This speech was on a Conservative Opposition Day motion, proposing that the House condemn the so-called "Boycott, Divestment, and Sanctions" movement (BDS), which seeks to boycott all Israelis, even those not involved in politics. This was one of many speeches in which I reference my maternal grandmother of Jewish heritage who lived in Germany during World War II. Unlike other opposition motions which we put forward during my first year in Parliament, this one had the support of the cabinet and did pass. (Notably, the motion was opposed by the NDP and by a couple Liberal MPs, and many more abstained).*

*As an aside, you may note that I mention my daughter by name towards the end of this speech. Since my wife was playing this speech live back at home, I wanted to work in a little 'shout-out' to our young daughter. Especially during the early days of this job, my daughter has struggled with having dad away so much. We have a very close relationship, and she appreciates it when I work in a shout-out from time to time. It is a tangible reminder that, regardless of what else I am doing, she is always on her daddy's mind.*

Mr. Speaker, members of the House know, as I mentioned before, that my grandmother was a Holocaust survivor, and so I am particularly honoured to be speaking strongly today against contemporary discrimination against the Jewish people.

I am very proud to be a Zionist. A Zionist was defined originally as someone who supported the re-establishment, and now as someone who supports the development and protection, of the Jewish nation called Israel. There is for me an important connection between remembering the lessons of the Holocaust and supporting the modern Jewish State of Israel.

Zionism began at the end of the 19th century, but support for Zionism was not a slam dunk even within the Jewish community. Some liberal-minded Jews perceived in fact a tension between the call for a separate Jewish state on the one hand and the demand for full Jewish equality within existing European states on the other. They saw the call for a separate Jewish homeland as contrary to their project of seeking integration and assimilation.

However, the terrible experience of European Jews during the Second World War demonstrated for most Jews, and most non-Jews alike, the need for a Jewish homeland. As much as Jews everywhere continued to seek full acceptance in nations where they lived outside of Israel, the opportunity to go to an ethnic and religious homeland provided them and provides them with vital security. If and when things go badly, Jews always have somewhere to go. This was not the case at the time of the Holocaust.

My grandmother was part of a mixed family. They were only able to obtain one visa, so her father, the full-blood Jew in the family, left for South America. My grandmother and her mother had to stay behind without him. We all know the tragic case of the St. Louis, a boat carrying Jewish refugees from Germany, which Mackenzie King refused to allow into Canada.

Noting this experience, Jews have rightly reasoned that as much as they can hope for goodwill from other nations where they live, they cannot always depend on it. Israel not only has a right to exist, its existence is necessary. Without it, Jews will not have the security that comes with knowing that, if worst come to worst, they always have somewhere to go.

Despite some dark moments, Canada and Israel have had a strong partnership. Certainly, we have much in common. Of course, we disagree on some things. It is a misconception that those of us who are Zionists always agree with policies of the Israeli government. As the member for Calgary Heritage has said, "of course, like any country, Israel may be subjected to fair criticism, and like any free country, Israel subjects itself to such criticism with healthy, necessary, democratic debate." (*In House of Commons debates, you are not allowed to refer to each other by proper names, only by constituency names. The member for Calgary Heritage is former Prime Minister Stephen Harper.*) That self-criticism is part of what makes Israel a great nation: vibrant, open debate about politics between people of different philosophies and from widely varying religious traditions.

In Israel, the only liberal democracy in the Middle East, all citizens are able to run for government, to attend university, to hold any job, to sit on the Supreme Court, or represent their country on the international stage, just as Canadians are. Israelis, just like Canadians, can aspire to any goal and are free to work to achieve it. Frankly, Israel's Muslim population enjoy more economic, political, and religious freedom than do Muslim populations in many neighbouring Muslim-majority states.

Canada and Israel have much in common. We are vibrant democracies, we value multiculturalism, we protect the rights of all citizens, and we enjoy robust democratic debate in two official languages: for us it is in English and French, and for them it is Hebrew and Arabic. With these traits in common, it is natural for Canada and Israel to have a very strong bond.

Like Israel, Canada has spoken out in the past about global anti-Semitism, and we must do so again. Let us be clear: anti-Semitism and racism almost never identify themselves as such, but a movement that calls for boycott, divestment, and sanctions, not on the basis of actions, views, or words of the individuals facing the boycott but on the basis of national origin alone, is clearly an example of anti-Semitic racism. We have an obligation to speak out, not only in support of a friend, but to take a principled stand on something that runs counter to our deeply held values of diversity and inclusion.

We are fortunate to live in a country where we do not face discrimination on the basis of things like religion, sex, age, or ethnic or national origin. The Charter of Rights and Freedoms entrenches the fact that everyone is equal under Canadian law. This section of the charter reflects our deepest held values. People should not face discrimination on the basis of religion or of ethnic or national origin.

The boycott, divestment, and sanctions movement, or BDS, advocates for actions that run entirely contrary to these Canadian values. They advocate discrimination against individuals and businesses on the basis of national origin. BDS openly calls for discrimination against and boycotts of Israeli individuals, artists, companies, organizations, academics, universities, research institutions, hospitals, and technology and development projects, again, simply because they are Israelis. BDS advocates for discrimination against those who happen to be Israelis, and also against Canadians who hold dual Canadian-Israeli citizenship. BDS seeks to discriminate against individuals for no reason other than the passport that they hold.

George Santayana said that those who do not learn from history are doomed to repeat it. Boycotts against Jews have occurred throughout history, based on lies, misinformation, and prejudicial assumptions. We are now seeing boycotts against the world's only Jewish state, and against all citizens of that Jewish state. Is it plausible that this is really simply about a political statement, or is it not obvious that this is something much darker than political disagreement?

BDS does not advocate peace between Israeli Jews and Palestinians. On this side of the House we support negotiations between the Israeli and Palestinian leaders, and we support a two-state solution. However, instead of trying to bring people together and support meaningful collaboration, BDS seeks to silence dialogue and once again single out Jews and Israelis for ill treatment. These actions do not contribute to peace, they only drive people further apart.

Now this motion is one that I would have hoped would receive unanimous support from the House, and frankly, I am perplexed that some members are opposing it. The best that we hear from those who are disinclined to support the motion is reference to freedom of speech. It certainly does not restrict anyone's freedoms for this House to express its support for our collective values of tolerance and inclusion, and to express our opposition to discrimination on the basis of national origin.

In 2010, Maclean's magazine ran a cover story calling Quebec Canada's "most corrupt province". This House responded by unanimously passing a motion which expressed "its profound sadness at the prejudice displayed and the stereotypes employed by Maclean's magazine to denigrate the Quebec nation, its history and its institutions."

Earlier, in 2006, The Globe and Mail published a story about the shooting at Montreal's Dawson College, in which the author suggested that the province's history of linguistic strife contributed to the incident. Following that, the House unanimously passed a motion, "That, in the opinion of the House, an apology be given to the people of Quebec for the offensive remarks of Ms. Jan Wong in a Globe and Mail article regarding the recent Dawson College tragedy."

In these instances, members of all parties did not have a problem understanding that the House can express its opinion without limiting free and robust debate. As we must always ask in these cases, why treat Israel differently?

The collaboration between Canada and Israel benefits all of us. Just this past week, my daughter Gianna and I assembled our new SodaStream machine. SodaStream has a plant in Israel, which provides good well-paying jobs to both Israelis and Palestinians. Let us stand today against racism and anti-Semitism. Let us stand in support of tolerance and inclusion, and also in support of delicious fizzy drinks.

# DEBATING THE GOVERNMENT'S DECISION TO LEAVE THE FIGHT AGAINST DAESH/ISIS

## FEBRUARY 23rd, 2016

*This speech was given during a debate about revisions to the nature of our military mission against Daesh. Throughout, I use the term "Daesh" as opposed to "ISIS" or "ISIL", because that is the term generally preferred by its victims. Those looking for an enunciation of the primary arguments in favour of continuing the bombing mission against Daesh might want to move to the next speech. This speech focuses more on directly refuting the arguments made by government members, rather than on presenting new arguments. Because Members of Parliament are usually reading pre-written speeches, and often arrive right before and leave right after their speaking slot, direct and systematic refutation of previous arguments is rarely done. But I believe that the direct refutation of one's colleagues' arguments should be an important part of Parliamentary debate. If we do not take the time to examine and refute each other's arguments, then we are in fact talking past each other, rather than to each other. So here was my attempt, perhaps ill-fated, to talk to and persuade government MPs about a key foreign policy issue by directly countering their points.*

*This speech begins with a reference to 'time-splitting.' The rules of the House allow an MP to split their time slot with another MP. In order to do so, one must say during the body of one's speech that one is splitting one's time.*

Mr. Speaker, I have the pleasure of sharing my time with the member for Prince George—Peace River—Northern Rockies, whose good comments I am very much looking forward to hearing.

I have been listening to this very important debate over the last couple days and think I can maybe offer three distinct points about it and what it says about the mission in general.

First, I want to talk about how we are being offered false choices by the other parties. Then I want to talk about the lack of definition around what is actually going on in the mission and some of the terms that have been used to describe it and the situation in general. Finally, I want to talk more generally about the question of intervention, when we intervene, how we intervene, etc.

In terms of the first point about false choices, we have heard members of the government and the NDP talk about the importance of different things we should be doing in the region and, for the most part, I would agree with them. We have heard some good comments from our NDP colleagues about the importance of anti-radicalization, as well as the importance of addressing terrorist financing. These things no doubt should be part of a comprehensive approach.

The government has talked about humanitarian assistance, about helping refugees, and about training. These are all very good things as well, and on this side of the House in particular, we have emphasized the importance of the bombing mission, but more broadly than that, the importance of being involved in fighting Daesh, not just supporting those who are doing the fighting but actually doing some of the fighting ourselves.

More than that, I think what we have said is that there needs to be a multi-pronged approach that includes all of the things the other parties have been talking about. We believe in humanitarian assistance—the Liberals did not come up with that just now—and helping refugees, training, anti-radicalization, and addressing terrorist financing. These are things that we have all

26

been involved in for a very long time as a country. However, it is also part of our historic tradition to be involved in fighting evil, in trying to protect the innocent and being willing to to be there on the front line. This is the right thing to do and we have long tradition of doing it.

There has been discussion in this House of a multi-pronged approach. Our approach very clearly has the largest number of prongs. We all agree that there need to be multiple prongs in response to Daesh. What we are arguing against is what we see as a government trying to break off one of those important parts of the mission. It is a false choice. We are told we have to decide between training and humanitarian assistance, and being involved in the fight. We do not have to decide between those things. We can and should be doing all of them. That is our position on this side of the House.

Another false choice we are hearing is some members' comments about how Daesh will ultimately have to be defeated on the ground, as if somehow we have to choose between a response on the ground and a response in the air. Of course, Daesh has to be fought on the ground and of course it is important that we partner with local troops in the area that are fighting Daesh, but surely no effective ground combat mission can happen without some kind of support from the air. That much I should think is obvious, that any cohesive military response involves activity on the ground and activity in the air. Again, this is a false choice that we get from the government. We can be involved in the military component from the air as well as assisting training local forces on the ground.

We should not buy into these false choices as if we cannot be doing more than one thing at the same time. In fact, generally speaking, since these different parts of the mission are done by different parts of the government, it is not at all problematic to have different areas involved. Anti-radicalization, terrorist financing, these are things that are addressed either through law enforcement or at the community level. Humanitarian assistance, helping refugees, training, these are done by different parts of the government from those that would be involved in front-line fighting. We can be doing all of these things at once quite effectively. We have the capacity to do them.

The second point I want to make is that there is a real lack of definition around certain aspects of this mission. I recall a comment by the member for Surrey—Newton, who just spoke, the other day in questions and comments when he alluded to this as being some kind of peacekeeping mission. A number of other members have referenced the legacy of Lester Pearson in the context of peacekeeping, as if they are under the impression that these are people going into this region in blue helmets, which clearly is not the government's approach and clearly is not happening.

We have heard terminology around a humanitarian mission, around a training mission. There has been such a lack of clarity from the Liberal side on whether or not this is a combat mission. Whether or not we call this a combat mission has significant implications for the people involved, for the troops, because the kind of support they receive while they are there and when they get back home is informed by how we describe this mission.

There is such a lack of definition. There is such a soup of terms coming from the other side.

I recall another speech in which a member—I cannot recall which one—referenced Ricardo's theory of comparative advantage. The member who just spoke again talked about playing to our strengths. I do not know if they have thought through the implications of those kinds of arguments, because the implication of that argument is that being involved in the front lines, being involved in the bomber mission, is somehow not a strength we have.

I think that is a strength and we have a comparative advantage because of the effectiveness of our air force, because of the effectiveness of our women and men on the front lines. Therefore, the implication of that kind of statement suggests somehow that we are less able to do that than other countries, which is totally fatuous and frankly quite troubling.

We have all these terms floating around from the government without clear definition. I know we have heard the suggestion that somehow its approach is a more sophisticated one. I will say respectfully that perhaps it is so sophisticated that the government members do not even understand what the mission is all about, because we have heard so many different kind of things about the mission. They will have to get that sorted out, and they should be willing to answer some very basic questions about the nature of the mission.

There is another much more important area where there is a lack of definition. The members of the government are not willing to accurately describe the situation on the ground. The reason they are not willing to describe it accurately is that it has implications for how we would respond. Those of us on this side of the House have frequently pointed out that what is happening in Syria and Iraq right now is nothing short of genocide. The word genocide has been used by former secretary of state Hillary Clinton. It has been used in a resolution passed by the European Parliament. It has been used by many human rights groups.

Why is the government unwilling to call a genocide a genocide? The reason it is unwilling to use that word is that it understands that the use of the word genocide entails a responsibility to protect. It entails a responsibility to respond in a much more serious way than the government is willing to do it.

If the government is fully confident that it is doing all it can do and that it is doing the best it can do, then why not use the word and describe the situation accurately? We see, in the unwillingness to use the word genocide to describe a genocide, a tacit admission that Canada is not willing to own up to the responsibility entailed in this idea of responsibility to protect. Therefore, we have a lack of definition both in terms of this mission and in terms of the actual situation happening on the ground.

As my final point, I want to address questions of intervention in more general terms. Often when we talk about Canadian troops being involved in a conflict in the Middle East, there is some discomfort, which is maybe people looking at past conflicts and wondering if we are getting into a similar situation.

There has been some discussion in this House about Canada's involvement in Libya. Nobody has pointed this out yet, as far as I have heard, but there was general agreement within this House about the mission in Libya. Liberals, and I think even New Democrats at the time, voted in favour of Canada being involved in a bombing mission in Libya. In retrospect, we can certainly say that what happened in Libya did not end up the way we would have hoped. However, that is a mission that all of us own, to some extent.

However, there are some important differences between the situation with the Daesh and the situation in Libya. For one, we are not going in to overthrow an existing government without a strong understanding of who we are fighting in support of. In fact, we are working very closely with an existing Iraqi government and with existing Kurdish forces. We are supporting ground troops, so we are involved from the air, but we are doing it in concert with troops on the ground. That is the best possible recipe for success.

There are many examples of intervention gone badly, but there are also many examples of non-intervention gone badly. I can think of cases where terrorist groups were left in power far too long and were able to wreak havoc as a result.

These are important points to consider: the government is offering us false choices in this debate; there has been a general lack of definition; and the questions of intervention should point us in the direction of getting involved in a multi-pronged way in this case.

Canada has a long tradition of being willing to stand up for our values in armed conflict, and we should do it in this case.

# HOW TO DEFEAT TERRORISTS
# IN IRAQ AND SYRIA

DECEMBER 10th, 2015

*This was my second speech in the House of Commons. It was given on a Conservative Opposition Day motion which called for the continuation of the Canadian bombing mission against Daesh. Of the three speeches given on this topic, this is the one where I most clearly and specifically explain why the fight must be continued.*

Madam Speaker, I have been listening with great interest to today's debate, and it is a real honour to be able to contribute to it as well.

I want to outline what I see as the three principle arguments as to why the motion should pass and why our involvement in the bombing mission in particular is important. First of all, we have a moral obligation to protect the vulnerable. Second, maintaining our collective security commitments is critical for our security. Third, bombing Daesh is a necessary part of our anti-radicalization efforts. I am going to talk a bit about those three things in the time I have today.

First of all, we have a moral obligation to be part of the bombing mission in order to protect the vulnerable. I spoke about this in some detail in my maiden speech, but I am going to talk again about that briefly before I go on to the other points.

What is happening right now in Syria and Iraq is nothing short of genocide. We have used that word on this side of the House, and certainly that has not been contested by any other parties. Genocide has never been quite so visible, so undeniable.

Even the Nazis did not broadcast their atrocities on television. When it came to past atrocities, many of us could have perhaps said, if only we had known, then we would have done more. That cannot be said in this case. We all know what is happening in Syria and Iraq. There is no denying it. If we have not watched the videos, then we know that they exist.

I hear what the other members are saying. They are saying that we should perhaps help the vulnerable but we should do it in a different way. I have a hard time taking those arguments seriously because they do not seem to respect the urgency of the problem. We can educate people to address potential violence. We can train them to address future violence. However, if we want to stop the current violence, then we need to fight as well. It does not mean that there is nothing else we can do to contribute positively at the same time.

The approach we on this side of the House advocate is a multi-pronged approach. We support being involved in education, the humanitarian response, training, as well as fighting. Talking only about those more long-term aspects of bringing about peace and stability in the region, to me sounds a lot like fixing the locks once the thief is already inside the house. Stop the violence; protect the innocent, and then by all means do more. However, there is an imminent threat, a present campaign of violence and genocide, and it will require more than words and social programs to stop it. We need to do something right now. We need to respond right now. We need to protect the innocent. We need to do what we can to stop the violence. We have a moral obligation to protect the vulnerable.

Second, I want to talk about maintaining our collective security commitment because this is crucial for our own security. The party opposite has talked about how during the last election it had committed to withdrawing from the fight against Daesh, but surely it can see that things have changed since the Paris attacks. Canada and France are both signatories to the NATO treaty. Article 5 makes it clear that an attack on one NATO ally is an attack on all.

Short of the formal invocation of article 5, it is still critically important that NATO members respond together. Russia and other powers are already testing the resolve of our NATO alliance. When events like the attack on Paris take place, it and others will be watching to see what we do. It is essential for global security, and for our own security, that NATO members stand and respond together to an act of war against a member state. A strong united response from NATO would show our resolve, would deter aggressive behaviour from other actors, and would keep our people safe. A non-response would do the opposite.

Canada has already been attacked, right here in this place, by Daesh inspired terrorists. However, what happens if we are attacked again, in perhaps a more coordinated fashion, and then on the basis of our collective security commitments we ask our NATO allies to be part of a response? What are they going to say to us? Are they going to say that they will send some blankets and do some training behind the lines? I hope not. Collective security is important. It is the basis on which we stand. It is how we protect ourselves in an environment where we do not have the capacity to oppose the world's largest aggressive powers alone. In addition to the other reasons already given, participating in this bomber mission is how we show that we take collective security seriously. I have said that we have a moral obligation to protect the vulnerable, that maintaining our collective security commitments is critical for our own security.

Finally, I am going to talk about how bombing Daesh is a necessary part of the anti-radicalization effort. We hear a lot from others in this place about deradicalization. However, strangely, we rarely hear them actually define the radicalization that we face. If we are going to talk about deradicalization, we have to have a good understanding of what kind of radicalization we are up against.

Let us be clear. Daesh is a deeply ideological organization. It is thuggish, violent, and evil. However, we should not infer from these things that it is thoughtless. Its members are thinking about how to enact a very particular and most would agree very misguided version of Islam. Whatever we call it, Daesh is a religious group, with particular beliefs that we would do well to understand if we care about deradicalization.

Daesh is trying to recreate an imagined eighth century caliphate, a caliphate that applies a particular conception of Islamic law, and, necessarily, that caliphate has certain very particular requirements for its existence. A caliphate is a particular form of religious organization, understood in various different forms of Islamic political thought as encompassing both religious and political control. In particular, it ruled by a caliph, thought of to be the successor of the prophet Muhammad. Many different Muslims look in their history to the idea of a caliphate, and there have been different caliphates with different kinds of legacies, most of them, of course, looking nothing like Daesh, the so-called Islamic State.

The last caliphate, the Ottoman Turkish caliphate, was headquartered in Istanbul. It disappeared in 1924, after it was ended by Kemal Ataturk as he turned Turkey into a secular state. For some Muslims, and many of those who are not Daesh supporters, the existence of the caliphate is theologically very important and they look to its eventual re-establishment.

Daesh represents the most serious attempt to resurrect a caliphate in almost 100 years. The particular school of thought that Daesh belongs to would identify a number of key conditions for a caliphate to exist.

First, the caliph must be a Muslim adult male Qureyshi, which means a member of a particular Arabic tribe to which Muhammad also belonged. Second, the caliph must demonstrate good moral character. Of course, many would dispute that the current proclaimed caliph, al-Baghdadi, meets these conditions, and certainly many Muslim theologians have argued persuasively that his actions are essentially anti-Islamic and immoral. However, in the eyes of his followers, he has met these conditions. He certainly is Qureyshi. In any event, there is not very much we can do to convince them that he does not fit conditions one and two. The third, and perhaps most important requirement for a caliph, is that he must have authority. A person who meets conditions one and two but has no army or territory is still disqualified from being a caliph unless and until he acquires territory.

This House needs to understand that Daesh is trying to enact this fantasy. Its members are not just thugs; they are thugs with a particular religious agenda.

This history is important for our motion today because the most important thing we can do to counter radicalization is to take away Daesh's territory. Without territory, even in the eyes of its followers, it will cease to be a caliphate. We need to wreck this fantasy. We need to show vulnerable men and women who might be susceptible to the arguments of the radicals that there is indeed no real caliphate to join. We need to do this, and, frankly, we need to do this right away. The longer the supposed caliphate exists, the more persuasive the arguments of its boosters will sound.

Daesh is not al-Qaeda. Al-Qaeda is a para-state organization that hopes, at best, to pave the way for the emergence of a caliphate. It did not have anything near the ambition of Daesh. However, Daesh is seriously and ambitiously evil. It is playing for keeps, and we do not know what hell we are in for if we do not stop this madness now.

I have two young children. I want to be able to tell them that we got the job done and we did not leave this for generations to come. We have a moral obligation to protect the vulnerable. Maintaining our collective security commitment is critical for our own security. Bombing, defeating, and destroying Daesh is the necessary step toward effective anti-radicalization.

# MAIDEN SPEECH

DECEMBER 8th, 2015

*It is funny how the way I prepare for a speech has changed so dramatically and so quickly. A couple of the speeches contained in this book were given extemporaneously, with very little advance warning. In other cases, I made detailed notes. But this, my first speech, was written out verbatim, and then repeatedly practiced and revised with the assistance of dear wife Rebecca. Nowadays, I often forget to even tell her when I'm giving a speech.*

*As my first speech (what has come to be known as an MP's "Maiden Speech"), this was a deeply personal project. It was an opportunity to share key elements of who I am and what I believe, and to make an argument for some of the things that most centrally motivated me to run for office. This was a speech given in reply to the Speech from the Throne. The Speech from the Throne is the very general statement at the beginning of each Parliament of the government's priorities. Given its general nature, there is a great deal of latitude for speeches given in response. One can, in fact, speak on any public issue which is related to something discussed in the Speech from the Throne.*

M r. Speaker, as this is my first speech in the House, I would like to express my gratitude to the people of Sherwood Park—Fort Saskatchewan for the trust they have placed in me.

I want to give particular thanks to my parents. Today, my father is celebrating his 60th birthday. "Happy birthday, Pop".

Also, I especially thank my wife, Rebecca, and our children, Gianna and Judah, for their love and support. I think that practising speeches with my two-year-old heckling me about her desire for a snack is pretty good practice for speaking in the House. Judah was born less than two weeks before the campaign started and so it has been a busy time for our family. My wife, Rebecca, has already sacrificed far more than I have to make this possible.

I am very conscious as I stand here today of the sacrifices that were made by my parents and grandparents to give us the best they could in life. In that vein, I will start my speech by talking about the experience of my maternal grandmother, the greatest influence on my life outside of my parents, and someone whose experience is particularly relevant to one of the debates we are having.

My grandmother was a refugee. She was born in Germany in 1930, the daughter of a Jewish father and a gentile mother. Hitler came to power in 1933 when she was three years old. She and her mother left Germany for South America in 1948 when she was 18, after a childhood that, frankly, was not a childhood at all. She met my grandfather in Ecuador, a Canadian engineer who was working for Syncrude, which explains how they ended up in Alberta.

All members in the House from all parties are deeply moved by the plight of refugees, myself in particular because of my family's experience. Therefore, out of genuine concern for those affected by the unfolding tragedy in Syria and Iraq, and also out of concern for our own national well-being, we must ask the current government hard questions about its refugee policy.

How will the Liberals ensure that the most vulnerable refugees, members of religious and ethnic minority communities who often cannot get access to refugee camps, are actually included?

How is the government going to ensure that it is only victims of violence and not perpetrators of violence who are coming to Canada? Profiling on the basis of gender and sexual orientation is not a reliable way to screen out extremists.

Most essentially, given the proportions of the current unfolding crisis, how is the government proposing to deal with the root cause, the ongoing civil war, and the emergence and growth of Daesh? People on the ground, members of diaspora communities, and all Canadians want to understand what the government is actually thinking here and why.

The Liberals say that sending fighter jets is not the best thing and that Canada can instead contribute in other ways. Really? Of course, Canada can contribute in other ways, but our bombing mission against Daesh has been extremely effective at reducing the amount of territory it controls. This sort of mission is, after all, the reason we have an air force, to protect ourselves and to project our values, and to use military force to protect innocent women, children, and men.

Now is a good time to re-ask a question that was asked and not answered in the lead-up to the election. If not now against Daesh, then what possible case is there in which the current government would ever authorize military action?

The Liberals say that they are withdrawing from the bombing mission because it was an election promise, but they have not been shy about breaking other election promises. They promised that 25,000 government-sponsored refugees would arrive before the end of the year. However, now they will only be admitting 10,000, and most them will be privately sponsored. Their justification for breaking this promise was that they wanted to get it right. It is no small irony, in light of many of the comments made during the campaign, that getting it right meant abandoning their refugee targets and coming close to adopting ours.

However, if getting it right was the justification for shelving the government's refugee promise, we would humbly suggest that the Liberals also get it right in the fight against Daesh and stand behind an effective military mission that actually defends the defenceless.

We need to be welcoming refugees in a responsible and effective manner. What refugees in the region want, even more than to come to Canada, is to have a country that is livable again.

What is the real reason for the government's planned non-response to an unfolding problem of violence against the innocent? It has yet to give any explanation for its planned withdrawal other than the clearly very thin arguments already mentioned. I do not think its response would have satisfied my grandmother or any other refugee of past or present conflicts. I do not think it will satisfy the 25,000 we may eventually take, and it certainly will not satisfy the millions who will be left behind.

At the root of this practical question is a moral question, a question about the kind of people we are and about whose lives we think are worth fighting for. Neville Chamberlain, the arch defender of appeasement, said in 1938:

"How horrible, fantastic, incredible it is, that we should be digging trenches and trying on gas-masks here, because of a quarrel in a faraway country between people of whom we know nothing..."

"People faraway of whom we know nothing". At the time, my grandmother was just eight years old.

On this side of the House we believe that the lives of the people of Iraq and Syria matter. The lives of the 25,000 we may eventually take and of the millions who will be left behind matter. It is not important how far away they are, they share a common humanity with each of us. What is implicit and consistent across many different contexts in the statements of the appeasers, the non-interventionists, and of those mealy-mouthed inbetweeners who pursue the same policies without giving their reasons is the implication that those in the immediate path of an evil power do not matter enough for us to bother getting involved. Even if, to our shame, we wish to look away, the menace still spreads.

After World War II many people said of the Holocaust "if only we had known, we would have done more". When it comes to Daesh, we know. We have genocide in progress, live broadcast over the Internet. We would not be worthy of the name civilization if we chose to do nothing about it. No good person likes a fight but the lives and security of Yazidis, Christians, Kurds, Turkmen,

Shia Muslims, and other groups in the path of Daesh, the 25,000 we may eventually take, and the millions left behind are worth fighting for.

It is a great honour to serve in the Parliament of such a great nation. I quoted Neville Chamberlain on his case for disengagement so I will balance that out with a quote from Winston Churchill who said, "The price of greatness is responsibility". I urge the government to take that seriously. We are and we remain a great nation, a nation that need not come back because it never left. When it comes to doing its part, we are a nation that has never before turned away from responsibility.

# HOLOCAUST MEMORIAL DAY

## JANUARY 27th, 2016

*As I have outlined in my Maiden Speech and elsewhere, much of my concern about international human rights is informed by the experience of my grandmother. I had the opportunity to deliver a statement on behalf of our party on Holocaust Memorial Day. In this brief statement I highlighted my own personal connection to the Holocaust and also emphasized the importance of fighting evil in our own time.*

M r. Speaker, today is Holocaust Memorial Day, a day when we remember the six million Jews and many others who were killed by the Nazis.

Many of my relatives were among the victims. My grandmother, a half-Jew living in Germany at the time, survived but not without suffering the loss of her grandparents, cousins, and many friends.

My relatives could have left Germany earlier, but stayed behind because they did not believe that such unspeakable evil was possible in their civilized society.

As uncomfortable as it may be, the Holocaust forces us to contemplate evil and how we respond to it. We must never be afraid to call evil what it is. When we say, "Never again", it is time we mean it.

Fighting evil had a cost in World War II and it has a cost today. My grandmother was always grateful that Canada was prepared to pay the cost in her time.

Let us be firm in our resolve when we say, "Never again".

# ON THE PASSING OF MANMEET SINGH BHULLAR AND ON AFGHAN REFUGEES

DECEMBER 8th, 2015

*One of my first meetings after assuming the role of Deputy Critic for Human Rights and Religious Freedom was with a leader in the Sikh community. We spoke for about an hour and a half about many different issues. During that conversation, this leader alerted me to the terrible situation facing Sikhs and Hindus in Afghanistan. I was told that Manmeet Singh Bhullar, a former Alberta cabinet minister, then an opposition MLA, had been leading the charge on this issue, so I asked my staff to set up a meeting for us to discuss the issue. Manmeet died tragically in a car accident before we had a chance to meet. Below is a statement I made in the House, to both honour Manmeet, and to highlight the challenges facing religious minorities in Afghanistan. At the time of writing, the government has not taken any action on this issue.*

Mr. Speaker, our Alberta Conservative family has lost a giant. Manmeet Singh Bhullar was a big man with a big heart.

In what turned out to be one of the last causes he ever took on, Manmeet championed the cause of Afghanistan's increasingly desperate religious minorities. At one time, Afghanistan had around 200,000 Sikhs and Hindus. Today, they number less than 10,000. Security concerns have even prevented some Sikh children from attending school.

The Canadian government can help Afghanistan's religious

minorities by creating a special program under section 25 of the Immigration and Refugee Protection Act. This has been done in the past, and communities in Canada are ready to step up if the government takes the necessary steps.

To honour Manmeet, but also because it is the right thing to do, I call on the government to take the necessary steps to help persecuted religious minorities living in Afghanistan.

# PART 2
# OUTSIDE THE CHAMBER

# RELIGION AND FOREIGN POLICY

## APRIL 29th, 2016

*Edmonton-area conservatives have set up an excellent initiative: the Edmonton Conservative Speaker Series. This is a monthly event that brings conservatives together to hear a speaker on a current issue. It tends to alternate between elected officials (at various levels) and conservative-minded academics or representatives of third party groups. In some cases, speakers may be quite critical of conservative parties - the series is not just about getting conservatives together; it is also about making them think. This is a speech I gave to the Edmonton Conservative Speakers group on April 29th, 2016. I spoke about the relationship between religion and foreign policy.*

I appreciate the opportunity to speak today on a topic that I believe to be of great consequence.

When we talk about almost any topic at all, it is common and a bit cliché to say that "the world is changing". Cliché because, after all, the world is always changing. What is interesting about the foreign policy situation we face in the 21st century is not, actually, that the world is changing. It's rather the fact that the world isn't changing, even if we would like it to have, or would like to think that it had. But I'll come back to that.

As you know, I am the Deputy-Critic for Human Rights and Religious Freedom for our caucus. We recently had a debate in the House on the renewal of the Office of Religious Freedom, and our motion to renew its mandate was voted down.

Just for purposes of a quick overview, the Office does 3 main things. (1) It provides training to the public service. (2) It does direct advocacy – speaking out about and bringing attention to the plight of persecuted religious minorities. (3) It funds direct on-the-ground projects with local partners in various countries, projects which advance religious freedom. (This is where most of the office's modest $5 million budget goes).

Evan Solomon wrote a piece for Macleans about the Office after that motion in which he defended the Office's work. I actually don't know where Evan is personally on matters of faith or theology, but he had an observation in this piece that I think was quite poignant, and also notable because it used an analogy that will be uniquely appreciated by many modern western audiences.

He said "In politics, religious is like sex – everyone does it, and nobody talks about it."

And this, I think, is quite true. When it comes to religion – most people 'do it' in some form or degree – some people do it more often or take it more seriously, different people do it in different ways, but our general sense that it is not a thing discussed in polite company doesn't make it any less a part of our lives.

I often hear from people who think religion should not have any place in politics. And they may be right, and they may be wrong – but the fact is that, to the extent that it does currently have a place in our politics, then surely it is sensible to note its presence and to talk about. Because, as with sex, sometimes the refusal to acknowledge a contributing factor in a situation can have very negative consequences for our ability to understand it.

Now religion is undoubtably a fairly limited factor in politics in the western world, compared to what it has been historically. Many western nations 'do religion' but they also don't treat it that seriously. For many of us in the west, religion is like an odd sculpture they we inherited from our grandparents – kind of nice, a little weird, but generally harmless. Maybe we put it on the mantle, or maybe we leave it in a box, but we don't have the heart to throw it out. We might even pay special attention to it on

1 or 2 days every year – but making significant sacrifices for that sculpture or spending large sums of money to have it restored, or voting for a political candidate based on their appreciate of this sculpture, these things would seem a bit disproportionate.

But we need to appreciate the fact that for the vast majority of the world population, and the vast majority of people throughout the swath of human history, this diminutive role allocated to religion even by many of the faithful would seem totally absurd. We may have changed, but in this respect the rest of the world has not.

Religions are, after all, not just sculptures or arbitrary rituals – they are systems of thought (of varying degrees of coherence) which seek to describe who we are, what we are, why we are here, and what we ought to do. Religions are systems of thought which seek to answer, or at least make intelligible, almost every question of any significance. So of course religion matters – and those who treat religion like it matters are probably onto something, given what it actually is. Certainly there is some logic to the typical non-western assumption that religion is important, in contrast to the typical western attitude – the blasé and largely un-thought-out assumption that it does not.

Why are hundreds of thousands of people dying in inter-community or state sanctioned religious violence around the world? Western liberal commentators are often quick to tell us that it really has nothing to do with religion – that it's all about something else. You've heard these arguments before – the rise of ISIS is really the result of Climate Change, the execution of Egyptian Christians in Libya can be better explained by poverty – since it was poverty that drove them to go to Libya in the first place, cases of communal violence in India are really just people looking for a scape goat (which is itself a religious idiom), the increasingly subtle but ever present suppression of Tibetan Buddhist in China is just politics, the seizure of churches by the Erdogan government in Turkey is a power grab unrelated to the stated Islamist inclinations of that government, the successful coopting of the

Russian Orthodox Church is an isolated and arbitrary effort unrelated to Putin's overall plan, the decision this year of thousands of Pakistanis to stand to honour the life and so-called martyrdom of a man who murdered a local politician because he spoke out against Blasphemy Laws – perhaps they only came to the funeral procession because the weather was nice, thousands of westerns have fled to join ISIS because they are indoctrinated fanatics simply moved by bloodlust. Western commentators are oddly eager to always tells us that none of these things really deep down have anything to do with religion.

This effort to avoid taking into account the role of religion in current world events obviously stretches the bounds of credulity. When we see people all over the world – in most parts of the world, doing good things, or bad things, or neutral things, to, for, and against people of the same or different religions, while pointing explicitly to religious ideas and texts to justify them, shouldn't we at some point acknowledge that, whether or not we want to talk about it, religion matters in today's geopolitics? Again, the point is not so much that the world is changing – it's that the world isn't changing.

Now this hit home for me in a particular way during a recent trip to India – the birth place of a number of the world's great religions, and home in some sense to virtually all others. Hinduism, India's principle religion, is in fact better understood itself as a family of religious ideas than as a singular religion in the particularly western sense. And India is a country where religion matters greatly.

Now Hinduism teaches samsara or re-incarnation – the idea that you are likely to come back again in a future life as something else, and that your chances of being re-incarnated as something better are shaped by your ability to live out the Dharma or purpose of your particular position. Westerners generally have fairly romantic ideas about re-incarnation, but there is a dark side to this belief – it is the fact that re-incarnation can imply that people who are born to privilege deserve that privilege and that people who are born to suffering deserve that suffering. This idea is the basis of the justification for India's caste system – a system of ranking individuals which continues to have powerful affects on Indian society, despite the best efforts of the government.

Now caste is a western term, which covers two interacting concepts called Varna and Jati. Some of you may be familiar with Varna, which are the macro castes – and there are 4. (Brahman, Kshatriya, Vaishya, and Shudra) – and a 5th who don't get a caste, who are beneath the caste system – who are sometimes called Untouchables, or who call themselves Dalits.

While I was in India, I had the honour of meeting one of the leading Dalit activists – a recently elected BJP Member of Parliament, Dr. Udit Raj. And it was such an honour to talk to him about his work over the years. He said that the caste system is the greatest evil known to man – it is a system of racial and ethnic discrimination, fundamentally bolstered by religion. And certainly with a much longer history than any other particular system of racial or ethnic discrimination.

Now I do want to be very clear here – there is a lot to admire about Hinduism, and also about the way many Hindus are now standing against the evils of the caste system. Hinduism, in philosophy and in practice, is also very diverse - but caste-ism is still in a certain sense a religious idea. Considering another example, while ISIS is not representative of Islam, its ideas are certainly religious of a certain kind. It has been interesting for me to discover in fact the residual impacts of caste in other faith traditions – there is no denying that caste has impacted relationship and dynamics within the Christian community, as well as other communities.

But, despite the efforts of many Hindus to confront caste, and despite the reality that caste does have some residential impacts within other communities, it is perhaps understandable that large numbers of lower-caste Hindus have converted to other religions in recent years. And this has resulted in some degree of 'conversion panic' in certain quarters of Indian society. Religious conversion by lower-caste Hindus to other faiths has, of course, the potential to significantly change the religious demographics of India.

Now given India's colonial history, it is understandable that many in Indian society might be concerned about widespread conversion to the religious traditions of previous colonizers – and there are frequent efforts to cast conversion in colonial terms – other, sometime foreign backed interests, using coercion to try to lure un-educated people towards Christianity or Islam.

There may be cases where unsavory tactics are used to encourage conversion, of course, but the social and economic incentives for lower caste Hindus seem to overwhelmingly point away from conversion to other faiths. India has a system of "reservations" (what we would call affirmative action) for lower caste Hindus, which helps them access education and opportunity. Despite the enduring negative impacts of caste-ism in India, it needs to be underlined that much of elite and official India does a great deal to counter this system. But "reservations" are not available to Christians and Muslims from lower caste backgrounds, even though they face the double-discrimination of being a religious minority and from a lower caste. This entrenched discrimination is particularly odd given that reservations are available to lower-caste converts to Sikhism and Buddhism, even though those religions also reject the caste system. (There certainly are separate human rights issues which concern the Sikh community in particularly, although these are probably too complex to explain in the time I have. I will note that, like Alberta, Punjab is place where it's almost impossible to find anyone who voted for the current government).

The practice of denying reservations to lower caste Christians and Muslims was defending to me by a different Member of Parliament I met with, on two bases – he said that converts have access to specific benefits that come with being part of a religious minority. It was not, however, evident to me that such benefits exist in any substantial sense. But also, the point was made that caste is a Hindu problem, and that those who convert are no longer within the caste system. There is some truth to this, but lower caste Christians and Muslims still are identifiable as members of lower castes, still bear the legacy of millennia of discrimination, and still often face residual caste-ism even within their own new-found religious communities.

So there are strong incentives NOT to convert, but many lower caste Hindus still do, I can only assume generally for philosophical as opposed to material reasons. So, in light of the 'conversion panic' that this has induced, some Indian states have responded by introducing perversely-named 'freedom of religion' acts. These are laws which do not forbid conversion, but require someone to seek the approval of a local magistrate before doing so. The justification for this policy is that it ensures that conversions are 'real' and not the result of pressure or inducement, but it's not obvious how local state officials, accountable to a deeply religious Hindu public, are best disposed to assess the credibility of someone's conversion away from Hinduism. This requirement obviously imposes significant practical barriers for anyone wishing to convert.

So this is a problem – a problem of religious discrimination, but also of caste-based discrimination, because implicit in the arguments in favour of these so called 'freedom of religion' acts is the idea that many lower-caste people are not sufficiently educated or wise to make decisions about their own religious practice without someone else's supervision.

Another important thing to understand about the religious/political interface in India is the role of the RSS, and the associated role of the BJP.

When I was in India, I met with a wide range of religious, political, and human rights leaders, from different traditions and political backgrounds. If I remember correctly, all of them but one raised, unprompted, the role of the RSS in Indian society – and the one who didn't mention the RSS was actually someone who I knew to have been a very active member of the organization.

The RSS is the world's largest voluntary organization, with 5-6 million members. It does voluntary work, has social activities, etc – and its orientation is Hindu Nationalist. It represents 1 of 2 dominant visions of Indian society. The secularist vision highlights India's status as a secular country with many different influences and traditions. The Hindu Nationalist vision views India as a pluralistic Hindu-majority country – which of course it is – but the emphasis is put on India's Hindu heritage, and a desire to preserve that.

There are always problems with these kinds of comparisons, but this distinction might be best understood by noting how, in Canada, some people would highlight our status as a secular country, while others would wish to underline that we are a pluralistic country with Judeo-Christian roots. These visions are not incompatible, but they do have different emphases.

Wikipedia describes the RSS as a 'paramilitary' organization, which is not entirely correct and not entirely incorrect. It is really an umbrella group of many different affiliated organizations, many of which have been involved in inter-community violence at certain times. The RSS itself was once banned during British rule, and has been banned at 3 different times since – and it was a former RSS member who assassinated Mahatma Gandhi. It is, in my view not unfairly, seen as playing a key role in fomenting community tensions which too often express themselves in violence. The RSS isn't the Klu Klux Klan, but it's not exactly the Rotary Club either. Like India itself, the RSS is big, is complicated, and has many faces.

The BJP, India's Hindu Nationalist Party, which now governs India, is effectively the political wing of the RSS. Incidentally, one thought I had while in India was that wouldn't it be great if we had a strong conservative social and cultural organization that was affiliated with our Conservative Party – though not one, I hasten to add, which operates too much like the RSS. Because of this arguably questionable affiliation, it is understandable that the rise of BJP is a matter of concern for many religious minorities in India. Regardless of the intentions of the top leaders in the current BJP government, the rise of BJP is perceived (probably not incorrectly) as creating a more permissive environment for Hindu militants. The election of the BJP was also accompanied by an effort to introduce a national "freedom of religion" law, an effort which was ultimately unsuccessful. And, religious minorities are closely watching the government's plans to reform the education system, wondering if this will result in the re-orientation of the curriculum in a Hindu nationalist direction.

On the other hand, what is exciting about India's now no longer that new government is that Prime Minister Modi has a very impressive record when it comes to economic development in Gujarat, and from a cultural perspective, comes from a lower-caste Hindu background.

I mentioned earlier my meeting with Dr. Udit Raj – a leading Dalit activist and now Member of Parliament. He is not a Hindu – he is one of many Dalits who have converted to Buddhism. He is also, though, a member of the BJP, although he had previously led a smaller party of his own. I asked him how it is that a Buddhist would be a member of the BJP. He was quite frank about the pragmatic need to be part of a major party in order to have an impact – but he also said that the BJP is best positioned to address the problem of caste discrimination if it wants to – because of the RSS. This massive affiliated social and cultural organization has the capacity to change hearts and minds, in a way the public policy cannot on its own.

Now I hope you've found this background on India interesting in its own right, but it also underlines the importance of religion in geopolitics. Our understanding of India, the relationship we have with India, has to be informed by understanding of the religion/politics interface. We could, of course, choose to ignore human rights entirely, but if we are going to speak constructively into human rights situations around the world, then we have to understand the religious roots of conflict, and the religious roots of regional or cultural pathologies.

India is a democracy, where any argument we would make is already being made by strong civil society organizations, but we can lend our voice, in an informed way – and we can support those on the ground working to counter these problems.

I say we, not as the western world generally, but Canada in particular. A US delegation on its way to India to study issues around religious freedom was recently barred from getting a visa. Despite my own stated interest in human rights and religious freedom, the Indian government was very helpful to me during the visa process, and helped to facilitate certain meetings. Because of strong people to people connections and shared history – and the fact that we are not a global super-power, these things give us an opportunity to speak into the situation in India, but also elsewhere in a particularly effective way.

While in India, I also travelled to Dharamsala, the headquarters of the Dalai Lama and of the Tibetan government in exile. We did not specifically discuss the Office of Religious Freedom, but the Dalai Lama highlighted the importance of Canada playing a role in the debate around Chinese human rights. He noted that, because we don't have any conflicts with China, we can speak about these issues from sincere motivation, and we can highlight our own domestic experience.

I also really appreciated the opportunity to meet with members of the Tibetan Parliament in Exile. These are people who go through the challenging process of getting elected, and yet because of the Chinese occupation, their Members of Parliament have absolutely no control over public policy. Imagine it! A system of government in which Members of Parliament have no control over public policy.

Now an Office of Religious Freedom helps ensure that we are addressing vital human rights issues in a way that is informed by the realities and the underlying pathologies on the ground. It is how we deal with the root causes of conflict.

But we have a government that is now turning its back, not only on religious freedom, but on international human rights more generally. The foreign minister was recently in Burma handing out money, and made no mention of the significant and growing persecution of Burma's Rohingya Muslims. When I raised the issue in question period, it was not obvious to me that the Parliamentary Secretary even knew what a Rohingya was. And, while the US Administration, the US Congress unanimously, the British Parliament and the European Parliament have all recognized the genocide faced by Yazidis and Christians – our government has refused.

And perhaps this is another topic for another day, but I think a big part of why the government is stepping back from an emphasis on the situation of religious, ethnic, and linguistic minorities around the world is because, while nation states vote in the security council election, persecuted minorities do not. I do want Canada to have a seat on the Security Council, but not at any price – not as the only crowning objective of 4 years of a foreign policy which is more interested in winning a popularity contest than in standing by our values.

We owe it to our belief in the universal dignity of all human beings to have a foreign policy which looks past nation-states and sees people who are suffering – and that digs deep enough into that suffering to ask why.

# CONFRONTING IRAN'S GROWING AMBITIONS

FEBRUARY 2nd, 2016

*An Ottawa event brought together members of the Iranian and Jewish community to discuss Iran's growing influence and the recent nuclear deal. In these short remarks, I lay out very specifically my response to certain questions about how the potential tension between principle and practicality should play out in the current Middle East.*

*In retrospect, I still very much like this speech; but, I worry that I was not sufficiently clear about the importance of an absolute dedication to the protection of human rights. One reading of point number two could be that short term human rights can be sacrificed in the pursuit of long term human rights gains. I do not believe that. I do not believe that those intrinsic rights that are owed to all human beings ought to be treated as anything other than absolute and inviolable. But the point remains that we need to have some form of relationship with certain states which, though bad on human rights, are a likely bulwark against worse abuses of human rights. That is the point I am seeking to make here. I am not suggesting that violating human rights is ever acceptable; rather, that dealing with states that violate human rights is permissible provided that the advancement of human rights remains the primary objective.*

Good Evening – Thank you for the opportunity to be here today, and I appreciate the opportunity to bring warm greetings on behalf of our caucus and our leader Rona Ambrose.

I have the opportunity in my role as the Deputy Critic for Human Rights and Religious Freedom to speak to many different communities, and it's particularly exciting for me to be able to speak to an event here where different communities are coming together for a shared conversation.

And I want to pay tribute to the immense contributions made by the Jewish and the Iranian communities – to Canadian society, and to the development of global civilization. So much of religion, philosophy, arts and culture, etc have its roots in Jewish or Persian thinking.

I will just apologize at this stage as well for the fact that I have to leave shortly after my remarks – I'm speaking at another event this evening.

Now the question that I was asked to address today is Canada's relationship with Iran – in light of the Nuclear Deal, and also in light of the broader context in the Middle East. And to do so in 5 minutes or less.

In that light, I want to make 4 specific comments about Canadian foreign policy in this regard.

1. There is always a tension in our Canadian foreign policy – a tension between the moral dimension and the economic dimension. The Liberals are currently working on improving our relationship with Russia, China, and Iran – nations with whom we may have economic interests, but also nations which have very troubling human rights records. My view, and I think the majority view within our party, would be that we must prioritize our values, over economic considerations. We should work from the assumption that who we are, and being true to who we are, has to matter more than the benefits of a warmer trading relationship. Prioritizing values over dollars doesn't mean that we don't trade, but it means that we refuse to dampen our criticism even if a nation threatens some kind of negative economic response.

2. In addition to the tension between the moral and economic dimension, our foreign policy debates often see tensions between

short and longer term moral considerations, and these are inevitably much harder to balance.

The Iranian government is effectively engaged in a cold war in the Middle East, with Saudi Arabia and most of their Sunni gulf allies. In that context, it has to be pointed out that the human rights record of Saudi Arabia is in many ways much worse than the Iranian government`s record – the recent execution of Nimr-al-Nimr again indicating a disregard for basic human rights and certain recklessness when it comes to Saudi Arabia`s own security. Yet we have a relationship with Saudi Arabia, and we sell them arms. The argument for this engagement is rarely made in clear terms – but the reality is that, for all its faults, Saudi Arabia must survive. If the Saudi monarchy collapsed, we would likely be headed for a Syria-style civil war, in a country where ISIS is already operating – but this time a civil war where possession of world`s largest oil reserves and Islam`s holiest sites is at stake. Such a situation would be a human rights catastrophe.

While tensions between human rights and economic wants should always be resolved in favour of human rights, tensions between combatting short-term human rights abuses and attending to the longer term protection of human rights should generally (though perhaps not always) be resolved in favour of the long over the short term.

3. The present situation in the Middle East has created some rather peculiar alignments, and perhaps caught the Western world on the wrong side. I was in the Middle East over Christmas – I`ve been to Israel before, but this time I was in the UAE. The UAE, Saudi Arabia, and their gulf allies are evidently no friends of Israel. Yet these days the Israelis and the Saudis and other gulf states share their most important foreign policy priority in common – countering the growing influence of the Islamic Republic of Iran. All are very opposed to the Nuclear Deal.

The fact that historically divided nations in the region all agree that the Nuclear Deal presents significant problems should give us significant pause. It is easy to understand why both Israel and the gulf Arab states are concerned. Regardless of the affect that this deal will have on Iran's pursuit of nuclear weapons, it will undeniably free up resources which can then be used to fight moderate rebels in Syria, strengthen Hezbollah, exacerbate tensions in Yemen, etc.

On this question, we have most of the West and Iran on one side, and Israel and most of the Muslim world on the other.

4. The ultimate goal of our foreign policy in this respect should be to reconcile Iranian aspirations with the needs and aspirations of all members of the global community – but not just with the West.

The talks which led to the current agreement were P5+1 – the US, the UK, France, China, Russia, and Germany. No formal representation from other nations in the region. I wouldn't push this analogy so far, but this is sort of like negotiating the future of Czechoslovakia without having Czechoslovakia in the room.

So called "Peace in our Time" is only possible if it starts with peace in the region, and that means a dialogue which also stops the incitement of violence against Israel and the destabilizing of the gulf region. As part of such talks, the Iranians might well ask for concessions from Saudi Arabia – concessions for their own Shia minority and openness to a peace deal in the Yemen that gives the Shia minority some degree of genuine autonomy. And these would be good things.

We cannot disconnect the nuclear question from the broader question of the Iranian government's respect for peace and stability in the region. Nor can we disconnect it from the question of the rights of the Iranian people. We in the West can fully join hands with the Iranian government, when they show due respect for their own people and their neighbours. And I would content – not before.

So these are my observations, I regret that I cannot stay to chat after the event – but as I engage in these issues, I would encourage you to get in touch with me to share your feedback and advice.

Thank you and God bless.

# DIVERSITY AND RELIGIOUS FREEDOM IN CANADA AND INDIA

MULTIPLE DATES IN JANUARY, 2016

*In January of this year, I decided, somewhat impulsively, to spend a week in India. I did not go as part of any delegation – I just went, and asked my staff to book some meetings. My assistant, Daniel Schow, basically became nocturnal as he, a couple months into his first political job, worked to book me meetings and speaking engagements in a country on the other side of the world. As a result of his remarkable efforts, I spoke to students or faculty at four universities, and met leading human rights activists, MPs, and religious leaders – most notably the Dalai Lama. I gave some variation of this speech at three of the four universities where I spoke. Most of the speeches in this book are about foreign policy. But this one is something different – it is an example of 'doing' foreign policy. That is, it is a case of me speaking directly to people in another country in a way that is aimed at advancing Canadian foreign policy objectives. (Canadian foreign policy objectives, that is, as I would like them to be, coming from the opposition). Recognizing the various human rights challenges in India, I saw great value in speaking to students – and offering them arguments rooted in the Canadian experience.*

T hank you for that kind introduction. It is an honour for me to be able to speak today. I'm going to speak for about 45 minutes. I'll start by setting the stage, in terms of the Canada-India relationship more generally, and then talk for a bit about religious freedom, and that will give us a lot of time for questions and discussion.

It might be rather curious, at first blush, to say that the Canada-India relationship is of critical importance, simply because of how far apart we are geographically. We are, quite literally, on opposite ends of the earth.

Christopher Columbus got North America and India mixed up, but very few people have since. You might be interested to know that it is because of that mix-up that members of Canada's Aboriginal population were for a long time called 'Indians', and the term lives on in some of our legal language.

When Christopher Columbus first came to North America, he thought he was in India because he had a fairly limited conception of how big the world actually was. But if Christopher Columbus were to arrive in Canada today, there would be other things to add to his confusion.

South Asians – Canadians who trace their ancestry to India, Pakistan, Bangladesh, Sri Lanka, or Nepal – make up about 5% if our population. They include many politicians – the mayor of Alberta's largest city, Canada's ministers of Defense and Industry, and many other people of significant influence at different levels. My predecessor as the MP for Sherwood Park and Fort Saskatchewan, Mr. Tim Uppal, served as Canada's multiculturalism Minister, and was the first turbaned Sikh to serve in Cabinet outside of India.

And not just in politics – South Asians are leaders in Canada's economic and cultural spheres as well.

Despite the many very serious contributions of Canada's South Asians, though, I think the most well-known and recognized South Asian Canadian is still Indo-Canadian comedian Russell Peters. (Do we have any Russell Peters fans in the House)?

The fact is, despite geographic differences, Canada and India are looking more and more like each other. We have spoken a common language for quite some time, and the use of India's indigenous languages in Canada is increasing. We share a system of law rooted in English Common Law – although notably, Canada's French speaking province also uses Civil Law. And Canada's Indian community are shaping our continuing cultural evolution. Diwali, Eid, and other such holidays more common in India are increasingly celebrated alongside tradition Christian, Jewish, and other civic events in Canada – and even our Christian celebrations are increasingly shaped and enhance by the contributions of South Asian Christians. In the last month, I had an opportunity to attend Diwali celebrations and Christmas celebrations on Parliament Hill. Notably, both were organized by groups from the South Asian community.

The term we often use when talking about the connection between Canada and India is that we have very strong 'people to people' ties. The growth of Canada's Indian diaspora, along with the growth of communications technology, has meant the growth and maintenance of strong personal relationships between people in our two countries. Growing people-to-people ties, more so even than strong government-to-government ties, open the door for expanded cultural and economic integration. Trade between Canada and India has been increasing, and our nations have been working hard towards a free trade agreement.

On the trade front, we have just had a change in government in Canada, and my Conservative Party is now in opposition. Although I think it's fair to point out that my party has demonstrated much greater support for expanding free trade than any other political party in Canada, I am hopeful that the new government will continue to support improving Canada-India trade and will work to bring free-trade negotiations between our two countries to a successful conclusion very soon.

I would be remiss not to mention, in the context of the ties between Canada and India, my own personal connection to this great country. My wife's family hails from Goa. Without going into too much detail, I will just say that I learned a lot about Indian culture during our dating/courtship process. I had seen a few Bollywood movies, but even those could not prepare me fully. My now father-in-law, who has been a great help in my various elections, would tell voters "don't worry – I checked him out much more than you ever will, and I still let him marry my daughter".

In addition to the things I've already mentioned, Canada and India have the common experience of working to build strong and cohesive nations in the context of great internal diversity – and of doing so democratically.

We are not alone in this, of course – most of the world's democracies are becoming increasingly diverse – for instance, like Canada, the US and the UK have growing diversity, and a growing South Asian community in particular.

But it seems to me that both Canada and India enjoy greater recognition and appreciation of the success of their own particular approach to multiculturalism than do the US, the UK, and many other democracies.

I think this may be, at least partly, because both nations were multicultural from the moments of their founding. Multiculturalism in the UK, for example, is often thought of as a political choice – the UK could have chosen not to be multicultural, and there are still some who think it should have made a different choice. But for Canada and India, rejecting multiculturalism was never an option. If India hadn't been willing to be multicultural, in some sense, there wouldn't have been a united India. And the same is true of Canada – we were, at the moment of our founding, seen as the amalgam of 2 founding peoples, French and English. Without some sense of multiculturalism, or at least biculturalism, we would not exist as a people.

At our founding, we were French Catholics and English Protestants, but also many English-speaking Catholics, immigrants from other parts of Europe and the United States, Aboriginal Peoples, and what we call 'Metis' – a cultural group made up of descendants of Aboriginal Peoples and early French visitors to Western Canada.

The idea of a nation conceived on that broad a basis was a challenging one, at the time, but perhaps still today. The idea, for example, that you could have genuine democratic debate in a place where not everyone spoke the same language. Especially, the idea that people with very different world views, rooted in very different faith traditions, could embrace a common civic nationalism.

John Locke, the 17th Century English political theorist, was generally favourable to religious toleration, but he opposed it for Catholics and for Atheists. (Illustrating the potentially significant gulf between Catholic and Protestant thinking, at least as they were thought of in the past. He would have been skeptical of Canada's chances of succeeding).

Catholics were not worthy of religious liberty, Locke thought, because they were "loyal to a foreign prince". In other words, because they belonged to a Church headed by the Pope who was also a temporal ruler in central Italy. Atheists were thought unworthy of toleration because, according to Locke, they lacked a basic moral foundation. He wrote "Promises, covenants, and oaths, which are the bonds of human society, can have no hold upon an atheist."

These are principal arguments against religious freedom that you still hear made today – that people of certain faiths will be disloyal to the state, and/or will not abide by a common moral code.

But, even if only as a matter of history, Locke was clearly wrong. Catholics in Canada and India have been proud and obedient Canadians and Indians – while retaining their Catholicism and their connections to the Pope. Likewise, Muslims and Sikhs in both countries have sought to be loyal to their traditions and to the religious authorities to which they subscribe, while also embracing a shared civic nationalism and a general broadly shared set of national values. Locke didn't just make a theoretical claim – he made a historic one, about the way certain religious minorities would behave. And, it was a claim proven wrong by yours and our experience.

Now I mentioned the presence of diversity at the moment of our founding in both of our societies, but both societies have also become increasingly diverse over the course of time. And this allows critics of religious liberty to suggest that certain religious traditions are allowable, but that there are others which do not properly fit.

There are those who would say, for example, that Judaism, Catholicism, and Protestantism are part of the founding ethic of Canada, but that Sikhism, Hinduism, or Islam are out of place. There are those who want to distinguish between India's indigenous religions on the one hand, and faiths like Islam and Christianity on the other which, it is argued, came to India as a result of colonialism and still grow through conversion. The effort is made by some, and this follows Locke's criticisms of Catholicism to some degree, to suggest that certain religious systems are alien in the soil of a particular country or place.

But again, these arguments ignore history and are disproven by it. The history of Sikhism, Hinduism, and Islam in Canada, or of Christianity and Islam in India, reach back a very long ways, and most of those who practice these religions in Canada or India are very much also citizens of the place where they live. Although my wife's ancestors probably converted to Catholicism as a result of Portuguese colonialism, they are proud believing Catholics, whose religious community is also deeply shaped by a pride in the unique traditions associated with their South Asian identify.

In our two countries, multiculturalism in general, and religious freedom in particular, have been proven to work. As I work to defend religious freedom, it is useful to be able to say that the arguments against it have been proven wrong by the relative success of the Canadian and Indian experience.

Of course there are still challenges, in both countries, and I will talk about those later on, but the challenges can be overcome by acknowledging the successes that we have achieved up until now.

After being elected, on October 19th of this past year, I was assigned by the leader of our party to the role of Deputy-Critic for Human Rights and Religious Freedom. So it's my role to speak, in particular, about the importance of religious freedom, both at home and internationally. And, to do so at a time when religious freedom is under threat, perhaps now more than ever before. The arguments for religious freedom need to be made anew in every generation – because there are challenges to fundamental religious liberties, even in the very places where it has been most successful. That includes here in India, and that also includes in Canada.

In that light, I think it would be useful for me to take a step back, and talk a little bit about the intellectual basis for religious freedom – at least, how I see it, coming out of the Canadian context. From there, I will move to making a few comments about some of the conversations currently taking place in India, Canada, and elsewhere about religious freedom.

There are, I think, 3 foundational arguments for religious freedom. I will state them in what I think are increasing order of importance.

The first argument for religious freedom (and, I would argue, the least important one) is it's practical necessity. Regardless of principle, there is a real practical need to accommodate people of different religious views within any state that wishes to enjoy peace and prosperity.

A nation that denies religious freedom to its minorities will find itself frequently at war with itself, and likely in a situation of conflict with other nations who take up the concerns of ill-treated minorities. Religious openness, on the other hand, may allow religious minorities to be ambassadors with nations with whom they have natural connections, and make it easier for the host nation to form alliances, trade agreements, and broader confederations with others. And these things will allow the nation in question to find peace and prosperity.

I mentioned earlier Locke's concern about the divided loyalty of religious minorities. But minorities can help build connections which strengthen their home country and their community as well. Canada's relationship with India is a good example of this – the Indo-Canadian minority in Canada have helped to foster felicitous relations between our two countries.

It is no accident that nations who treat their minorities, and particularly their religious minorities well also find more friends outside their borders.

In both India's and Canada's foundings, we see how inter-religious harmony served a practical purpose.

In India, unity between religious communities helped make the fight against colonialism effective. The movement for India's independence was broadly conceived – for principled reasons, to be sure, but also practical ones. The tragedy of the violence that took place at the time of partition, on the other hand, tragically illustrates what can happen when there is a breakdown of religious harmony. One need not be deeply committed to religious harmony in principle to see that a breakdown of community relationships can be very bad in practice.

The deployment of religious liberty for political and strategic advantage can be seen repeatedly in Canada's history.

"Canada" was founded as a French and Roman Catholic colony, but it was conquered by the British in 1759, and secured as a British possession in the treaty signed in 1763 which ended the Seven Years War.

One of the particularly curious things about North American history is how, at the same time as relations were deteriorating between Britain and her English-speaking North American subjects in the so-called Thirteen Colonies (which became the United States), Britain managed to effectively accommodate French Catholics. Many have wondered how it is that accommodation worked with French Catholics, but not with more like-minded English Protestants. This is too complex a question to treat parenthetically, but it does suggest that people with different cultural and religious contexts may at certain points find it easier to work with each other than those who are more 'natural' allies.

French Catholics in the newly acquired British colony were able to continue to practice their religion, and were also allowed to maintain key elements of their legal and administrative traditions. The Catholic Church continued to play a prominent role in Canadian society.

British policies of religious toleration, it seems to me, were probably more based on practicality than principle. The British were not similarly tolerant of Catholics in the British home islands – particularly not in Ireland. Religious accommodation in Canada was a strategic move, more than a principled one.

In the end, it was a strategic move that paid off. When the Thirteen Colonies rebelled, a little over a decade after the conquest of French Canada, the rebellious colonies expected French Canadians to join them. They did not. The British had been relatively good to them, and they were not inclined to think that they would necessarily fair better in an as-yet undefined political relationship with English-speaking Americans.

Had it not been for the policy of religious toleration, Canada would probably have taken up arms alongside the 13 colonies, and been part of the newly formed United State of America. As a result of their policy of toleration, Great Britain retained a strong presence on the continent.

Of course, Canada today enjoys a very good relationship with the United States, but there were multiple points in our history after 1776 where attempted invasion either happened or looked very likely. And the regular threat of American invasion forced different elements of Canadian society, English, French, and Aboriginal, to work together.

In the so-called War of 1812, Americans thought they could take advantage of Britain's pre-occupation with Napoleonic France to invade Canada and chase the British from North America once and for all. Jefferson said that the invasion would be a "mere matter of marching". The British were indeed relative distracted. In the end, though, the Americans gained no territory, and we burned down the White House. Our success in that war was facilitated by a relatively positive relationship with Canada's Aboriginal communities, who fought alongside European settlers. And once again, the Americans thought that French-speaking Catholics would support their cause – but they didn't.

Now fast forward 50 years. Canada was founded in 1867, an unlikely confederation of British colonies in North America – bringing together, as I said, English Protestants and French Catholics, as well as peoples from all manner of other places and Canada's Aboriginal peoples. At the time, as had generally been the case up to then, there was fear of the possibility of American invasion. Invasion never materialized at this point – but the existence of that threat made an open broadly-conceived collaboration between different communities and different faiths seem to some like a security imperative. This strategic need for cooperation made the birth and success of this new nation much more likely.

Now here, in a nutshell, was the founding bargain which Canada struck – Canada was actually conceived as a relatively centralized federation. Our constitution gave authority over 're-serve areas' (areas not mentioned in the constitution) to the federal government. It also gave the federal government the power to disallow provincial laws. Intense centralization would have exacerbated the challenges of collaboration, but fortunately they never really materialized. In practice, for example, the federal power to disallow provincial statutes was never used, and was quickly revised out of existence.

Provincial authority was primarily in the areas of property and civil rights, and in the administration of social policy areas like healthcare, education, and welfare. Provincial control in these, at the time fairly limited areas, was important to Canada's Catholic minority. The province of Quebec, predominantly French and at the time predominantly Catholic, wanted power in these areas in order to ensure that the role of the Catholic Church in them would continue. At the same time, our constitution provided for the protection of denominational separate schooling across the country. Catholic religious schooling continues to receive full public funding in my home province, and in our most populous province, Ontario.

In 1867 when Canada was created, as a quasi-independent nation, the areas of social policy given to the provinces (education, healthcare, and most forms of social assistance) were considered to be of relative unimportance. The emergence of the modern welfare state, however, put these provincial social policy functions right at the heart of government activity. With universal public healthcare and education, suddenly the level of government providing these services mattered much more – and Canada is now, in practice, one of the world's most decentralized federations.

British and subsequently Canadian authorities, operating between the conquest of French Canada in 1763 and the confederation of Canada in 1867, were laying the foundations of a multi-cultural multi-religious state – but probably for strategic as opposed to high-minded moral reasons. They were developing accommodations which were politically necessary and strategically useful. Again and again, the religious freedom strategy proved successful. It allowed Canada to survive, and laid the foundations for its subsequent success.

Other nations would do well to learn this lesson from Canada's experience. In the world today, in an age where, as I have said, religious freedom is under attack more than ever before, we see how religious persecution is practically unhelpful for nations seeking to enjoy peace and prosperity.

We had a very clear example of this in the news last week.

Relations between Saudi Arabia and Iran weren't exactly felicitous to begin with, but Saudi Arabia undermined much of any hope of winning friends on the Shia side of the Middle East's emerging Sunni/Shia Cold War (hot war in some cases) when they executed popular Shia cleric Nimr al-Nimr. It is, I think, necessary to point out that al-Nimr was executed for alleged crimes against the state – his execution was a violation of his political and civil rights more so than his religious rights - he was not targeted simply because he was Shia. Still, he was very much associated with advocacy on behalf of Saudi Arabia's Shia minority. And, this execution clearly demonstrates how attacks on faith groups or religious leaders can undermine the strategic position of the nation doing the attacking.

This execution will almost certainly weaken Saudi Arabia's position in the region by (in my judgment unfortunately) pushing more Shias into the arms of the Iranian regime. In addition to weakening its position in the region, this execution will almost certainly damage Saudi Arabia's important (but already very fragile) relationship with the West.

Given significant Western concern about religious freedom, those who want to have positive relationships with the West will do well to provide basic human rights to their religious minorities.

Let us consider, in another case, China's poor treatment of religious minorities – Uyghur Muslims, Tibetan Buddhists, Falen Gong practitioners, and most kinds of Christians. Canada and other western nations vigorously debate the kind of economic relationship we should have with China. It is a complicated balance of principled concern for human rights and attention to our economic interests. But if China would only treat their religious minority better, they would largely take the human rights concern off the table, and we could proceed with pursuing economic integration with each other much more easily. China's ill-treatment of religious minorities makes it hard for them to pursue economic relationships with certain other nations.

Treating religious minorities well is virtually always practically efficious and strategically useful.

And certainly, Canadians, and particularly South Asian Canadians from religious minority communities, do raise issues around the situation of India's religious minorities whenever major developments in the Canada-India relationship are up for discussion. As mentioned, I am a big supporter of free trade between Canada and India, and it's worth noting that Canadian are generally more likely to be supportive of free trade with countries where they can be confident that we have shared values.

Three foundational arguments for religious freedom. Number one, religious freedom is a practical necessity.

Number two - religious minority communities have a basic and non-negotiable right to continue to exist.

Religious rights can be presented as collective rights – the right to exist and be recognized as a group; and religious rights can be present as individual rights – the right to identify with the religion of one's own choosing. For the purposes of this particular point, though, I will emphasize the collective or group dimension.

Religious groups exist as communities – groups of people with shared values and traditions. Religious freedom is about the rights of those groups to gather together, to act collectively, and to pass their collective values onto their children.

The collective expression of religious faith is the one most often attacked by extremists. Most tragically, we have seen the bombing of churches, mosques, synagogues, and other houses of worship during peak times of worship. We have also seen acts of vandalism against houses of worship, and public attacks on people wearing religious clothing.

Canada is not immune from this. In November of this year, following the attacks in Paris, a mosque in Peterborough in Ontario was damaged by a fire, deliberately set. Like any country, Canada has a small minority of people who don't buy into our broader vision of a tolerant multicultural society.

I am very proud, though, that in the last Parliament our government created a special fund to provide support to houses of worship for security upgrades (things like video cameras). In Canada, we have accepted that a society which respects freedom of religion must assume collective responsibility for the security of houses of worship – though these are private buildings, we accept in Canada that we have a shared public responsibility for ensuring their security, and we put our money where our mouth is.

There is concern here in India, and there is among your friends in Canada as well, about attacks on houses of worship that have happened recently in your country. In the last year, attacks on houses of worship and acts of violence against people wearing religious garb have occurred across India, and right here in this city.

When I have met with people in the Indian government about these issues, it is noted – and I think fairly, that India is a very big country, that these things are bound to happen from time to time, and that government is doing its best. I leave it to you to consider whether enough is being done or if more needs to be done to address these issues. Whether or not all is being done that can be done to protect houses of worship is probably to some extent a question for local and regional authorities, as well as the national government.

But I would simply like to take this opportunity to encourage you to embrace universal, collective responsibility for ensuring that people can worship without fear of violence. Because whether religious minorities are attacked by the state or attacked by rogue elements, the affect is the same – they lose the freedom to practice their religion collectively in peace and tranquility.

Freedom of religious obviously always does include the freedom to form a peaceful religious assembly – and to do so without fear that, even a large peaceful gathering of adherents of a particular faith will not be opposed or interrupted by the state. This is important here as well.

Three foundational arguments for religious freedom. Number one, religious freedom is a practical necessity. Number two, religious minority communities have a basic and non-negotiable right to continue to exist and to worship.

Number three – religious freedom is a fundamental individual, as well as collective right.

What, after all, is religion? Externally, it exists as a part of culture and community, a way of gathering together to worship God, as a way to pass traditions on to our children. This is the external visible phenomenology of religion.

But there's obviously something much more important going on as well. Religions are, at their core, worldviews – relatively cohesive systems of thought which make positive truth claims about the universe in which we find ourselves. People who are religious, and also people who are seriously non-religious, have often thought about what they believe, come to conclusions about what constitutes truth, and decided to act on that.

To think about our fundamental purpose, to think about our place in the universe, is so essential to the human experience. Thinking about who and what we are, thinking about what lies beyond ourselves, is what makes us different from animals. It's what gives us our dignity. I believe that our dignity is the product of our elevated status as beings who have a higher place and purpose, and have the potential to contemplate that higher place and purpose.

As a person myself who takes very seriously questions of our place in the universe, I can respect that others may have come to different conclusions than I have through the same process of serious thought – and it is their fundamental human right to do so. I believe deeply in their shared dignity, and therefore in the equal right of others to go through the same intellectual process that I have.

Religious freedom is the outworking of individual freedom of thought, it is part of our basic dignity as individuals. And that is why governments which deny religious freedom are always somewhat unstable – not just because they aggravate their populations and other nations unnecessarily – but because people who are told not to think, not to challenge, not to explore questions of ultimate meaning and purpose will always, at some point, look up into the sky and say "I have to know why" – and realize that they were made for something more than the blind acceptance of state enforced dogma. Our basic dignity as human being points us to always ask why – religious freedom is as basic as freedom of thought – it is fundamental to who and what we are.

Article 18 of The Universal Declaration of Human Rights explicitly makes clear this connection between freedom of thought and freedom of religion. In full, it says "Everyone has the right to freedom of thought, conscience and religion; this right includes freedom to change his religion or belief, and freedom, either alone or in community with others and in public or private, to manifest his religion or believe in teaching, practice, worship and observance."

This is the most important point, the central moral core of religious freedom – but it is also the part most attacked. Freedom of thought, freedom of religion as an individual freedom, means nothing at all if it doesn't include both the freedom to change your religion and the freedom to practice your religion as you wish.

Before coming to India, I spent some time in the United Arab Emirates (UAE), arguably one of the most liberal nations in the Muslim world – and yet a good example of how some have embraced this oddly bifurcated notion of religious freedom. In the UAE, the practice of faiths other than Islam is allowed to occur openly. However, conversion from Islam to any other religion is, at least officially, a capital crime. As a non-Muslim, I could freely purchase and consume pork or alcohol in the UAE, but the same law prohibits anyone who is Muslim from doing the same as me.

This makes sense, if you see religion solely as a matter of the rights of existing communities to preserve themselves – existing communities from other faith groups do better in the UAE than in almost any other country in the area. However, Emirates and other Muslims living in the UAE are not free to come to their own religious conclusions based on serious individual thought. They are not free to decide if they do or do not agree with the positive truth claims advanced by Islam, and they are not free to decide on their own interpretation of Islam if their interpretation goes outside certain limits.

In Canada (or here in India), someone might decide to be a Muslim, and also decide to eat pork. They might decide that, based on their own interpretation of Islam, eating pork is okay. Others might think that they were wrong, or in fact even not a Muslim. But the right to practice a religion "incorrectly" – to have an interpretation of one's religion which is regarded as heretical by the mainstream, is also part of religious freedom. This is pretty central to the individual-based notion of religious freedom endorsed by the Universal Declaration of Human Rights.

The obvious rejoinder might be that conversion, or more novel religious interpretation, could emanate from less than pure motives. A Muslim wishing to buy bacon in the non-Muslim section of a UAE grocery story might be doing so because they have a thought-out principled difference of opinion from mainstream Islamic scholars, or (perhaps more likely) they might wish to do so out of idle curiosity or in a moment of moral weakness.

Out of concern for people converting with impure motives, some Indian states have imposed laws which require prospective converts to seek the approval of local magistrates. The goal of these laws, as I understand it, is to ensure that people are converting for the right reasons, and not being coerced, bribed or manipulated.

Here are some of my thoughts on these laws.

Number one – people's basic right to freedom of religion is about the right to think and come to their own conclusions, and to do so in the way they wish. A person who wishes to keep their evolving religious convictions private, from the state and from their neighbours, has every right to do so. This, for the same reason that we have a secret ballot – the right to make religious or political choices includes the right to do so privately, because requiring religious or political choices to be public would limit some people from actually exercising their religious or political rights. There was a time before we had a secret ballot, but we moved in a different direction, for fairly obvious reasons. And, I think I'm on good ground making this case, since the Universal Declaration of Human Rights also clearly identifies a right to practice ones faith in public or in private.

Number two – whether or not a person converts with ideal motives is not the business of the state or of their neighbours. If someone converts, for example, from Hinduism to Islam, for unsavoury reasons - because they were offered money, or something like that – then they probably were never a very good Hindu and they will also not be a very good Muslim. So why, really, does it matter? If they are acting against their conscience, then they will bear responsibility for that before their own conscience, in this life and possibly the next. To convert for unsavoury purposes, to sin against one's faith and one's own convictions, is at worst a private crime – one not practically adjudicable by the state, and one on which the state has no need to adjudicate.

A person's thoughts can be corrupt or immoral, but they should never be criminal.

Number three – The potential for abuse of such laws is just too great, even if the original promulgation is rooted in good intentions. If a person is required to seek the approval of local authorities, themselves made up of religious people and democratically accountable to a deeply religious populace, it is hard to imagine that the religious convictions of local authorities would not play some role in the consideration of the petition to convert.

Of course, I think it is fair to point out that India's restrictions on conversion are not as significant as those which exist in many other countries. But protection of the right to change one's religion is really the test point of a nation's commitment to religious liberty. Many countries are failing this test – the existence of so-called apostasy laws in many different nations, in particular, is a serious affront to the universal declaration of human rights, and to principles of human dignity, broadly conceived.

I'd like to conclude my remarks today by ruminating briefly on one aspect of Canada's domestic debates about religious freedom, and I am eagerly anticipating the discussion we're going to have after that.

In the last federal election, religious freedom came up as a key topic of conversation. It did so unexpectedly, and I think quite by accident, and it was on a question of religious freedom that affects a relatively small number of people. But it was a question that galvanized particularly passionate disagreement on both sides.

My party, the Conservative Party, in government before the last election, decided to prohibit the wearing of the Niqab (full face covering which some Muslim women wear) during citizenship ceremonies. We were clear about doing that in a very specific context, and we did not and do not have any interest in broader Niqab restrictions.

Now I'm sure you can imagine, given my deep personal commitment to the idea of religious liberty, that the unique questions presented by the Niqab are things that I think a lot about.

Our political opponents said that this restriction on the Niqab was anti-Muslim. For what it's worth, I think this charge was clearly unfair – and it showed that our opponents either didn't really understand the place of the Niqab in Islam, or didn't have much interest in acknowledging nuance. It is, I suppose, often an unfortunate matter of course in politics that nuance is the first casuality of vigorous debate.

The claim that Niqab restrictions are anti-Muslim ignores the fact that the Niqab is actually more restricted in some Muslim-majority countries than it is in the West. In fact, it was a Muslim group in Canada – the Muslim Canadian Congress, which initially called for a full ban on the Burka or the Niqab – a much more extreme position than we would ever take.

What concerns some Muslims, and some non-Muslims as well, about the Niqab is the perception that women who wear them do not really consent to wear them – and that even if they do, the Niqab makes women's full participation in society more difficult. Further, some would see the Niqab as inherently anti-women.

On the other hand, the fact that the Niqab is a symbol of oppression in certain contexts does not exclude the possibility that some women who wear it are quite free from oppression – and choose to wear it freely and for their own reasons. Also, the fact that the wearing of the Niqab is very much a subject of debate inside Islam is not a sufficient reason to say that banning it does not constitute religious discrimination. In Canada, the test for a religious practice protected by religious freedom is "sincere belief" not "correct doctrine" – as I have said, it should be up to individual conscience, and not the state, to determine what is and is not a religious practice.

However, back on the other hand, there must be some practical limits on accommodation. A long standing Christian minority denomination in Canada called the Hutterites oppose photography, but are still required to have their photos taken for their driver's licenses. Showing your face and allowing your photo to be taken in certain contexts serves a practical purpose – in some cases of identification, but also of allowing observers to attest to the fact that an oath which is claimed to be taken is in fact being taken.

I would be quite curious to hear a bit more, during our question and answer time, about your thoughts on this question, and about how the Niqab is viewed and treated here in India. I note that, despite a very large Muslim population here in India, I do not think I have seen a single Niqab since arriving.

Although some issues on the religious freedom front are black and white, there are others which are more 'grey'. But the importance and success of the underlying principles – and the broad effectiveness of Canada and India at building multi-lingual, multi-cultural, and multi-faith societies, are not in dispute.

And it is by continuing dialogue about the importance of the underlying principles, as well as dialogue about these emerging 'hard cases', that we ensure a detailed understand of the importance of religious liberty. We can hope that dialogue like this will help to ensure that religious liberty continues to exist in our two countries, and that it comes to nations who have yet to embrace it.

Thank you again for the opportunity to speak today, and I look forward to your questions.

# ADDRESSING FALUN GONG PRACTITIONERS ON RELIGIOUS FREEDOM AND HUMAN DIGNITY

DECEMBER 3rd, 2015

*Falun Gong practitioners gather regularly on the lawn of Parliament Hill to draw attention to the persecution that practitioners face in China. In my first year I spoke at two separate Falun Gong events on the Hill. These are my remarks from the first one of those speeches.*

G ood afternoon. It is an honour for me to be here and to stand with you – in support of universal human rights, and specifically in support of your religious freedom.

Religious freedom has sometimes been called the First Freedom – because all human beings have a basic right and, in fact have a need, to understand their place in the universe. Regardless of the conclusions we come to - the process of reflecting on who we are, what we are, what our purpose is, and where we belong - that process is essential to what it means to be truly and fully human.

To be human is to look beyond ourselves, to ask and to answer those essential questions about who and what we are, and to be free to act on the conclusion we come to.

Now governments who restrict religious freedom are inherently insecure. They believe that this natural process of free thinking undermines social and political stability.

Free, unfettered contemplation is essential to the human experience. As long as a government seeks to reduce their citizens to something less than human, they will always be insecure, because men and women will look into their own minds and hearts and recognize that they were made for something more.

Friends, let me add, that the Chinese government has nothing to fear from Falun Gong. Those who are sincerely contemplating their place in the universe are not a danger to the society in which they live. Rather, those who are thinking seriously about who and what they are, their purpose, and where they belong will always be good citizens, because they will bring similar reflection to questions around their place in civil society. They will start with honest questions about how they fit in the universe, and continue with questions about how they can fit in and enhance civil society.

Frankly, those who reject or seek to restrict authentic spiritual contemplation are the greatest danger to the civic order. They deny the basic human dignity from which religious freedom emanates, and they act without thinking of the deeper questions of purpose, place, and value. State functionaries who behave like this are indeed a menace to the civil order.

When human dignity is denied, when contemplation, questioning, and disagreement are restricted, then corruption becomes rampant. And no aggressive punishment regime can replace a system in which people are thinking about where they belong and are thinking about what they owe to the spiritual and civil order in which they find themselves.

Corruption is defined as "impairment of integrity, virtue, or moral principle". So obviously corruption becomes endemic when honest contemplation and conversation about the nature and root of virtue and moral principle are restricted.

I have no doubt that China will one day see the full embrace of religious freedom – and China will be better, stronger, and more secure when that happens.

As conservatives, we stand with you – for your right to think, to be, to belong, to believe, and to act. You are true friends of a great nation, and we stand with you. Thank you, and God bless.

## PART 3
# SPEECHES ON
# RELATED TOPICS

# IN DEFENCE OF CANADIAN CITIZENSHIP

JUNE 3ʳᵈ, 2016

*These final two speeches are not directly about foreign policy, but they are important to this book because they discussed aspects of my political philosophy which are critical to foreign policy. The government has brought in a bill which changes a number of the rules associated with acquiring and maintaining Canadian citizenship. Most critically for the purpose of this speech, the revised rules would allow convicted terrorists to retain their citizenship. The principal arguments in favour of this approach suggest that citizenship is inherently irrevocable. To make citizenship revocable, the argument goes, is to make it conditional, and therefore to devalue it. In general, the rhetorical approach of the government in this context was to emphasize the importance and value of diversity. I argue here that diversity must be bounded, and it must entail shared principles. The same point that I make here about our domestic community is also true to some extent of the international community – we need to live together on the basis of shared values. Effective co-existence without some basic elements of shared values is extremely difficult.*

M adam Speaker, it is a pleasure for me to rise and address this important debate; and certainly an honour for me to follow my friend, the parliamentary secretary from Parkdale—High Park. I did not agree with much of what he said in his speech, but I appreciate his work in this place, and particularly the opportunity we have to work together on Parliamentary Friends of Tibet.

Before I get into the specific provisions of this bill, I want to spend a bit of time setting the philosophical groundwork, at least in terms of how I see it and many on this side of the House see it, on the substance of this debate, underneath these provisions, in terms of what Canadian citizenship is all about.

I will say at the outset that I believe that we live in the best country in the world. I do not say that lightly. I have lived abroad and I have travelled quite a bit. For many reasons, we live in the best country in the world. One of the proof points of that is the fact that we have so many people who want to come here. Over the last 10 years, we have had the highest sustained immigration levels in this country's history. However, comparatively as well, many more people want to come to Canada relative to our population than want to go to many other countries.

As we think about what our citizenship is and what it means, perhaps it is important to start by asking why Canada is such a great country, and what we can do to ensure that in the context of our ongoing definition and redefinition of citizenship we preserve what is essential about our country. We are all very proud of Canadian diversity. The parliamentary secretary spoke eloquently about the diversity that we have in this country. However, many countries around the world have diversity and perhaps have a different experience of that diversity. I was thinking as I prepared for this about the visit of the Chinese foreign minister. China is a very diverse country, but a country in which religious and ethnic minorities face significant difficulties. Russia is a very diverse country. Syria, in fact, is a very diverse country. So we have many countries around the world that are diverse where perhaps the experience of that diversity is not positive for those in the minority.

It is clear, if we look at this comparison, that it is not diversity alone that makes us great and it is not diversity alone that makes us who we are; but it is in fact what we do with that diversity, how we work together in the context of that diversity, and in particular our ability as a nation to build together around shared values. If we have diversity without any kind of shared values, there is always a risk of conflict. I am very proud of our history as a country that has both great diversity and has managed to maintain a strong sense of shared values. That is particularly important for our success.

It is worth underlining what some of these shared values are. We have a belief in this country in freedom. We have a belief in democracy, in basic principles of human rights and, to some extent, in universal concepts of human dignity that underline those ideas of human rights. We have a belief in the rule of law; in universal human equality and value regardless of race, religion, caste, ethnicity, linguistic background, et cetera. We have a belief as well in gender equality, which is very important to who we are in this country. We have unity around these common values in the context of our own diversity. Our experience of not just political unity, not just sort of general accommodation of one another, but of practical community and common purpose, is quite unique in this country.

I will just share this anecdote because it is important. I was in a European capital a number of years ago, meeting with a Canadian friend of mine who was working there. We were in a very diverse part of this city. There were people from all different parts of the world. We noticed around us all of a sudden that we did not see any mixed-race social groups. We saw a group of people from one racial group together, and then a group of people from another. We looked around us in the crowded centre of this European capital and it was a bit jarring to realize that in spite of the fact that this was a very diverse place there were no obvious signs of community, of at least people sitting together within that place.

The advantage we have in Canada is in building substantive community between different people of different backgrounds.

I thought about that experience later when, at the time I think it was the British prime minister, similar comments were made by French and German leaders, talking about the alleged failure of multiculturalism in the European context. As much as I would regard that as not correct, even in the context of Europe, it is worth understanding that there is a different experience of multiculturalism in Europe compared to the Canadian experience.

Canada, from the moment of its founding, was a country founded on shared values and on ethnic, religious, and linguistic diversity. We can compare that to many European states, which obviously emphasized elements of shared values, but also have measures of ethnic nationalism built into their founding as well.

We have to welcome newcomers in a way that understands that background without compromising what George Cartier called our concept of one political nation. I will read from a book called Straight Talk, which is a book on federalism that I captures this well.

"That dual quest for the universal and for cultural diversity has been with us since the birth of our Confederation. We have often strayed from it since then, and committed grave mistakes and injustices, but the result is this admirable human achievement that is Canada."

We have had this history from the beginning of combining the universal values in the context of diversity. The same book continues with:

"Finally, Cartier wanted Canada to be a "political nation", a nation of solidarity which transcends race, religion, history and geography to ensure that the French in Quebec would never want to break their solidarity with other Canadians. If we seek a contract at the birth of our federal union, it is certainly the one expressed by Cartier, which has inspired all of Peter Russell's work. Quebecers of all origins have helped other Canadians a great deal to achieve that ideal; they must not renounce it."

Straight Talk was written by the Minister of Foreign Affairs. I think he has had some very good things to say in the past about the importance of common values in the context of this diversity.

Where are we going from here then? What is the philosophy which underlines this legislation advanced by the government?

Early in the new government's term, the Prime Minister was

talking to the New York Times about aspects of Canadian identity. Here is what he said, which is something very different than the words I just quoted from the Minister of Foreign Affairs. He said, "There is no core identity, no mainstream in Canada...Those qualities are what make us the first post-national state."

Therefore, we have in the House, at least between our side and the Prime Minister, very different visions of what the Canadian nation is supposed to be.

Ours is one of unity around shared values in the context of ethnic, linguistic, religious, and other forms of diversity. However, the Prime Minister's concept is one that goes beyond or outside of this idea of shared values and emphasizes the diversity, but at the same time wants to perceive Canada as a postnational state, not as a political nation.

It is with that in mind that we come to legislation put forward by the government, which would allow convicted terrorists to retain their Canadian citizenship. I think we can understand what the Liberals' thinking is on this bill in light of the Prime Minister's comments to The New York Times and in light of that underlying philosophy.

It is clearly a problem to our historic concepts of Canada as a political nation to say that convicted terrorists should be able to retain their citizenship. A terrorist is not just someone who wants to do violence and mayhem. Terrorists are people, in our current conception of it, who disconnect themselves from our Canadian values, who embrace a wholly distinct set of values than the ones I have outlined, gender equality, universal human dignity, human rights, democracy, and the rule of law, and instead commit themselves to fighting for the destruction of those very values. A terrorist is not someone who is pushed outside of the fold of Canadian values. A terrorist is someone who chooses to leave the fold of Canadian values, and that is very clear.

Our concept of diversity that emphasizes shared values says that diversity does not extend to those who wish to destroy us. There have to be parameters or limits ensuring that we remain the country we have always been, a country of unity in the context of our diversity.

The Liberals view of diversity in many ways bends over on itself. It permits those who are deeply at odds with things in which the Liberals themselves clearly believe, gender equality, human rights, the rule of law, democracy. Yet it allows people who reject those things, who want to fight against those things, to remain in the Canadian family and to use the advantages of their membership in the Canadian family, of their Canadian passport, for example, to then wreck havoc against the very values that we espouse.

I think all of us in all corners of the House deeply believe in the idea of diversity, but we also believe the diversity is necessarily bounded as a practical matter, as a matter of our own survival. There are certain things we must agree are simply not welcome here and they include the desire to destroy our way of life.

I ask Canadians who are watching this to reflect on these differences of vision, the one espoused by the Prime Minister and the one espoused by George Cartier, the question of Canada as a postnational state or of Canada as being part of a common political nation.

It is important to specifically counter some of the arguments that were made by my friends across the way. Members of the government have said many things on this that are substantially true but do not really apply to this legislation. My friend, the parliamentary secretary, praised the importance of having a path to citizenship. We have always had a path to citizenship in our country. Nobody is proposing, or has seriously ever proposed, the creation of a sort of UAE-style of citizenship where an individual would have to be born here. We believe very much in a path to citizenship, and we can disagree over the difference of one year here or there in terms of being in a country without disagreeing on that fundamental point.

For those who have a commitment to Canada, there is no substantial problem with saying let us wait another year. Those who do not have a commitment to Canada will perhaps have a different perspective. All of those who have a commitment to Canada, whether it is an additional year, it is not clear to me what the breaking point is about those changes.

There is an important issue alleged by the government, and we hear this talking point many times, of two-tiered citizenship. There are two things that need to be said about this. First, the government has been clear that its intention is to retain the ability to revoke citizenship that was acquired on the basis of fraud. This means that people who acquired their citizenship could have it stripped from them on the basis of fraud.

Fraud is in my mind a much lesser crime than terrorism. For the government to say that on the one hand citizenship is irrevocable for someone who clearly parts ways with Canadian values and then say on the other hand, citizenship can be lost if someone cheated on a form is just not consistent.

If the government really takes this idea that citizenship is irrevocable to its logical extreme, it is hard to understand why it would be dealing with a more extreme issue, yet leaving in place the revocation possibility for a relatively less extreme offence.

I want to say this as well about the regime the government put in place. The government's bill would institute a system of two-tiered citizenship that did not exist before. Under its system, people who acquired their Canadian citizenship could have it stripped on the basis of fraud. Under our system, anybody could have their citizenship stripped on the basis of fraud or involvement in terrorism.

Under the Liberals' citizenship process, nobody who was born in our country or who was born with Canadian citizenship could ever lose their citizenship. Our system treats equally those who were born abroad and those who were born here. Therefore, I am perplexed by the Liberals continuing use of their talking point, in spite of their total unwillingness to actually implement the fullness of this supposed principle that they are espousing.

The fact is that where an individual was born does not matter for our original legislation. People could lose their citizenship if they were involved in terrorism, and it did not matter if they were born here or somewhere else. The value of Canadian citizenship is dependent on their commitment to our shared values, not on where they were born. That is an important principle and a principle for which we have stood.

Of course, as a practical matter, we cannot strip the citizenship of someone who only has one citizenship, and that is true whether individuals obtained their citizenship by a fraud or whether they obtained their citizenship in spite of then going on to commit or be involved in some form of terrorism.

That is a practical matter, and obviously we are limited in the House by certain features of the practical world in what we can do and cannot do. However, as much as possible, we should hold fast to that principle, that Canadian citizenship has value. It expresses the substance of who we are as a country, a country that has unity around shared values in the context of our diversity, and this, unfortunately, is simply not appreciated by the arguments made on behalf of the bill.

Some more clarifications need to be made about the original system we had in place. It is a bit perverse, frankly, that members of the government talk about new Canadians being worried about the provisions of the bill because of misinformation about them, and then go on to continually imply things about the bill that are incorrect. If some Canadians were worried about the provisions of the bill and did not have a proper understanding of what the original bill would do, I would hope the members of the government, who were maybe talking to these Canadians in the context of a campaign, would have provided correct information about the bill.

They might have clarified that actually there is no restriction whatsoever in the original Bill C-24 on mobility rights. There is no possibility whatsoever that people could lose their citizenships for a minor crime. In fact, people who commit a major crime, a violent crime, still could not have their citizenships revoked, regardless of where they were born, regardless of whether they were dual citizens. It is only in the case of terrorism.

The crucial point with respect to terrorism is that this is where individuals have stepped fully outside the parameters of Canadian values. They have said that they have no interest in being part of the Canadian family. They have acted in a way that put themselves fundamentally at odds with it in terms of their values.

One of the arguments we have heard as well from my friends across the way is the assertion that putting them in jail is enough, that someone should not face both imprisonment and then the loss of citizenship. However, these are two completely different kinds of sanctions to deal with different kinds of issues. Of course, somebody who is involved in violent crime or terrorism should be punished through incarceration, but there is also the issue of whether this person has retained his or her commitment to be part of the Canadian family or not. These are different issues that should be both dealt with and certainly both considered.

However, there is another practical matter that I think the government ignores in its reasoning. It is the fact that individuals could well be outside of the country and become very involved in terrorism, be fighting for Daesh, perhaps, or another terrorist group, and clearly, in the process of their actions and their involvement in that, take themselves outside the Canadian family. Those people, as long as they retain their Canadian citizenship, have the benefits of Canadian citizenship, can ask for assistance by diplomatic staff and Canadians would be on the hook to bail that sort of an active terrorist out.

Of course, we do not have the ability to incarcerate people if they are abroad fighting on behalf of another terrorist organization. This is perhaps a context in which this would have to be considered, and I do not think is properly considered by the government's arguments.

It is important to underline in that context at the same time that it is not the conviction in a foreign court that would lead to these considerations. It would only be a decision of the Canadian courts or an adjudication on the basis of equivalency, an evaluation that was done based on Canadian law with respect to terrorism. It still would not require someone to be in the country.

In terms of the underlying philosophy, Canadians should go with George Cartier, not the post-national anti-identity fantasies of the Prime Minister. It is also important to dig into the substantive provisions of the bill and realize that it does not fix problems that were real, that we were addressing significant problems.

# EUTHANASIA, CLOSURE, AND THE MEANING OF DIGNITY

MAY 3rd, 2016

*This speech was about a topic that may seem completely unrelated to foreign policy – euthanasia and assisted suicide. But this debate is very similar to debates around international human rights because both of these discussions require that we answer difficult questions about the nature and origin of human rights. As I've said before, human rights are inherently derived from human dignity. Concepts of what we are entitled to are only intelligible in light of some account of what we are. In this speech I ask the critical question – What Is Dignity? I seek to answer this question with an account of human dignity which also informs my views on domestic and international questions of justice and human rights.*

*Part of the context of this speech was the decision of the government to invoke so-called 'time allocation' or 'closure' on the euthanasia and assisted suicide bill. This means that the government was shutting down the debate before many members had had a chance to speak. So I speak both to the procedural issue here, as well as to the substantive one. This is one of seven different speeches I gave on this particular bill or on motions related to it. All of these speeches can be found online.*

M r. Speaker, because of the procedural direction now being taken by the government, I think this will probably be one of the last speeches in this debate.

I want to recognize the tone of the debate that has taken place. I know members have spoken politely, softly, and respectfully. This has been the tone on all sides. However, I wonder if I may stretch that tone a little bit.

This is the most important issue that Parliament will deal with, I suspect, in a very long time. Without resorting to personal attacks, this is an issue to get angry about, if there ever was one.

The mistakes that we stand to make in this legislation mean that men and women may die who would not have otherwise, who will be missed because of the absence of advance review, who will be pressured forward because of the lack of palliative care, and who will be matched with willing physicians because of allowances for doctor shopping, even if they have been identified as not meeting the criteria by their own and other physicians.

Tonight, we should be angry. Canadians should be angry. While speaking softly and politely about the need to talk about death and the need to listen, the government is proceeding to shut down debate after only two days. The invocation of closure in this case will not in any way affect the timeline of this bill. We know that.

It is already being studied at the justice committee, and even days of additional debate would not prevent the justice committee from proceeding on the timeline it has already set. A vote would not change that. It would not affect the timeline at all, and yet the government is proceeding to shut down debate with its notice of closure motion coming forward tomorrow.

Canadians who care about this issue from all sides, Canadians who care about the important role we have as legislators to examine and debate legislation in this House, these Canadians should be angry about what is happening on this legislation.

The absence of meaningful debate increases the significant chances of error when it comes to shaping legislation that is, in my view, already riddled with problems. An error on an issue this important will mean unnecessary loss of life.

I have already spoken about my substantive concerns on this bill, but by way of quick review, this legislation contains no meaningful safeguards because even the exceptions in it are riddled with holes. The written consent provision excludes those who cannot sign. The waiting period can be routinely waived. Mental illness is not at all clearly excluded.

The requirement that death be reasonably foreseeable is too ambiguous to effectively exclude anyone. The requirement that two doctors sign off merely encourages doctor shopping. Even if the already-ambiguous criteria are not followed, people who kill an unwilling patient can be let off the hook if they claim a reasonable but mistaken belief that the criteria applied.

I have said that we have here a perfect storm: ambiguous criteria and a reasonable but mistaken belief clause, which means that it would be nearly impossible to prosecute anyone who kills a patient, even without consent. We have heard the data from countries with similar systems and the impact they have on patients who do not consent.

All of these problems could be fixed through amendments. A requirement for advance review by competent legal authority would ensure that those who do not consent are not pushed forward against their will. Provisions on palliative care and conscience protection would better protect the autonomy of patients and would also protect the autonomy of physicians.

We could discuss these changes. We could make these changes. We ought to.

Tonight, I want to also do what other members in this House have done, and that is to share stories about life and stories about death.

My story starts around the turn of the last century in Germany, with a Jewish doctor named Rudolf Kuppenheim, the first person in his family who was able to get a university education. One day in the course of his practice, a young child named Gertrud was brought to him for treatment for diphtheria. At the time, the usual treatment was to make a small slit in the throat that would allow the afflicted child to breath. The child's mother, however, resisted this treatment. Her mother refused to allow Dr.

Rudolf Kuppenheim to make the necessary incision, because it would leave a scar. The mother believed that the scar would prevent her daughter from getting married.

Rudolf became angry, very angry, and justly so. He berated the woman for putting her daughter's life at risk. Notwithstanding the social pressures and the challenges that a young woman might face in that culture and time, this girl's life, her value, her dignity, were not dependent on whether or not she could find a husband.

As it happened, that girl not only got married, but she later married that doctor's son. That couple had a daughter who was born Ursula Lilly Kuppenheim, and Ursula Lilly Kuppenheim was my grandmother.

She grew up in a society that denied her dignity as well. As a half-Jewish child, she lived through the horrors of the Holocaust, only able to leave Germany after the war. Her mother had her dignity denied because she might have been hard to marry off. She had her dignity denied because of her Jewish heritage, but the shifting vagaries of social attitudes never changed who these women were: human beings.

Rudolf Kuppenheim and his wife tragically took their own lives when the Gestapo came to their home. Suicide is always a tragedy, but I understand that they were in a position where they felt that they had no other choice: suicide or tortured death in a concentration camp. No just society forces people to make that choice, but at the time my grandmother lived.

In 2006, my grandmother, or Oma as we called her, died of cancer. Everyone dies, but not everyone truly lives. Across continents, from persecution to extensive contribution, my grandmother truly lived.

She always told us that she wanted to die like Abraham, Isaac, and Jacob did. They did not suffer or get sick, at least at the time of their death. They just realized that they were about to die, called their families together, and said goodbye. That is what she wanted, but it did not happen that way. She did suffer very much.

Suffering is a part of the human condition. It is just and right that we seek to minimize it. It is also just and right that we understand that a human who suffers does not cease to be human, to have value, to have dignity. She had dignity from the moment she was born to the moment she died, whether her dignity was denied because of her Jewishness or because of her illness.

Members here have to understand that the so-called dying with dignity movement is shaped by a very dangerous view of humanity. It views human beings as instrumental or experiential creatures, valued for what they do or for the quality of their experiences, but that is not what we are. We are in fact creatures with intrinsic value.

We value the dignity of human beings, not principally because they are useful, because they are having a good time, or because they want to be valued. We value human beings because of what they are. We understand intrinsically the difference between human rights and animal rights, rights for creatures which have feelings and experiences only, and rights for creatures that have value intrinsically. This movement, this presumption that the ill or disabled lack dignity could not be more wrong.

I want to conclude with a final appeal to all members. If they have grave concerns about this legislation, stand up and vote against it at second reading. I know some members are worried about the possibility of a legal vacuum, but this legislation replaces ambiguous criteria with other ambiguous criteria. It does not create any kind of review mechanism. Fundamentally, it replaces one vacuum with another.

There is a better way. If members vote down this legislation or even ensure that the vote is closer, the government can, will, and indeed must come back with a more serious bill, and if it does a better job of incorporating certain specific proposals we have made, then we can all work together to ensure a quick passage of a better bill.

Alternatively, if we go along just because we want to proceed, we will have entrenched a piece of legislation that will cause real problems, life and death problems, problems that will be very hard to fix.

It is disgusting, but we have a proposal to invoke closure on an issue so vital, on an issue of life and death, after only two days of debate. We must stand up to this. We must make our stand. I have made mine and I ask members in the House to make theirs.

# CONCLUSION: POLICY RECOMMENDATIONS

In light of the challenges that the world faces, a clearly principled approach to foreign policy is needed now more than ever. Furthermore, a principled approach is required that is also judicious and strategic, and that plays to our strengths. There are contexts in which the insertion of Canada's principled influence could make a significant difference and could advance our strategic interests at the same time. As such, I would like to conclude this book with a number of specific recommendations for Canadian foreign policy going forward. I am not optimistic that these will be adopted by the current cabinet, given the pattern that we are seeing. However, I hope that these proposals will inform the ongoing discussion around Canada's foreign policy and see fuller realization under a future government.

1) Canada should leverage its significant people-to-people ties to make enhanced relations with India and Pakistan a major priority. Both of these countries face major challenges – challenges which our American and European partners don't have the same capacity to help tackle, because of either current superpower status or the legacy of colonialism in that region. Canada, without that baggage, and with strong people-to-people ties with both countries, can play a particularly constructive role working to counter discrimination, violent extremism, and other human rights problems. We can also strengthen economic relations at the same time. When seeking to address human rights issues in this region, we should always be constructive. Canadians can and should speak out publically on human rights at times, but helping Pakistan strengthen its public school system, for exam-

ple, would go a long way to preventing the increase of violent extremism as well. We are uniquely positioned to engage and work with India and Pakistan, in their own interests and in ours.

2) Canada needs to re-engage with Sunni Arab Muslim allies. Current American foreign policy has, unfortunately, de-emphasized relationships with existing Sunni regimes, in favour of collaboration with Iran. This is a dangerous strategy. Iran is a growing threat to global peace and security in a way that countries like Saudi Arabia, despite their faults, are not. We will be most effective in the fight against certain self-identifying Sunni Muslim extremist groups if we are working with Sunni Arab Muslim allies to the greatest possible extent. The government has shown some signs of interest in this; but, we must proceed in an open and transparent way. We can, and we should, work to build public support for this engagement – by explaining exactly what we are doing and why. The Liberal government recently hammered out a joint action plan to strengthen relations with gulf Arab states. This is a potentially good step, but the government has thus far refused to release the agreement. If there's no public buy-in on strengthening these relationships, then we're unlikely to get very far.

3) Relentlessly promote human rights in all of our dealings with every other state, including our friends. Do not single out our friends for criticism on human rights issues, but don't be afraid to talk to our friends about human rights issues either. As mentioned, I support constructive strategic engagement with Gulf states, and we need to be the kind of friend that tells it like it is and pushes on human rights issues. Fundamentally, there is no contradiction between working constructively with Gulf states while also urging them to fix their problems. The long-term viability of states like Saudi Arabia depends on their ability to reform; so promoting reform and working collaboratively are things that naturally go hand in hand.

4) Like with Saudi Arabia, we can and must push Russia and China to behave in more responsible ways. Both of these coun-

tries have significant domestic human rights problems; and, both governments are threats to international peace and security – Russia predominantly in Ukraine, and China in the South China Sea. I believe that we can find ways of talking to these nations that do not detract from a clear affirmation of our principles. Yet going forward, we must avoid the politics of 'reset', of public fawning, of giving concessions for nothing in return, and of standing by while a foreign minister berates a journalist for asking an appropriate and important question about human rights. These mistakes have all been made with respect to Russia or China in the first ten months of this Liberal government's term in office. Much is often said about the importance of 'face-saving' in Chinese culture. When we allow ourselves to be bullied, then we lose face and send a message of weakness. Being weak does not help us. It does not help us to address issues of moral concern, and it also does not help us to advance our economic interests.

5) We have to work with the Saudis and other non-radical Sunni Muslims to counter Iranian expansionism and violent extremism in the Middle East. Still, in the absence of further Saudi reforms, we must, where possible, seek to weaken Saudi influence in favour of more secular and liberal, or even more moderately conservative Sunni alternatives. This means working to strengthen the public education system in countries like Pakistan and exploring ways to limit the export of Saudi ideology more generally. It could mean playing a role in Yemen. Incidentally, international opinion needs to have a better appreciation of the importance of Yemen. If Yemen is eventually able to chart a peaceful course, involving Sunni-Shia reconciliation and the weakening of both Saudi and Iranian influence, it could become a strong example of what is possible. Alternatively, it could continue to foment Sunni-Shia tensions, and strengthen Saudi and Iranian leadership of each faction.

6) We need to face some reality in our relationship with Turkey. During the recent attempted coup, some western governments referred to the Erdogan government as Turkey's "democratically

elected" government. Serious problems in the most recent Turkish elections and the continuing abuse of civil and minority rights by the Erdogan government stretch the term 'democratic' quite a bit. There are no easy solutions on Turkey, but Canada and other members of the NATO at the very least need to start telling the truth about these problems.

7) In areas of general lawlessness, vulnerable communities often need more than our advocacy – they need training and arms. The government's policy in Syria and Iraq of providing training only to the Kurds misses the vital need to provide arms, training and support to religious minorities like Yazidis and Assyrian Christians as well. Their capacity to protect their own communities is the ultimate guarantee of their security and is a necessary check to ensure they are not betrayed by their neighbours. The conflicts between different groups are complex and it is not for us to define the exact shape of any future political settlement in Iraq and Syria, but it does not make sense for only some parties to have the means to defend their communities.

8) Canada should re-instate a focussed Office of Religious Freedom to engage on issues of religious freedom and the persecution of religious minorities around the world. The previous office was effective, building the capacity of the public service and ensuring the inclusion of a religious freedom lens for other activities, as well as providing direct support for projects on the ground. The government has noted that there are a range of other areas that are also important. I would see the value of creating similar, small, and highly-focussed offices within our foreign affairs department working on specific human rights issues. Issues like the rights of indigenous communities in other countries. Notably, when I was recently in India, I found that that there was great interest in learning from Canada's experience working with indigenous communities. We are far from perfect in this respect, but we have made a good faith effort at reconciliation and collective restoration. The humility with which we have collectively recognized the need for reconciliation is something that we can

talk about and promote internationally. But the lumping of very different kinds of issues into one office is a plan built to fail. Small, lean, focussed offices can work together, with the rest of the Department of Global Affairs, when it makes sense to do so. They can also become particular centres of excellence that others can rely on for information. We should build on the model of the highly successful Office of Religious Freedom. We should not destroy it.

9) Canada should have a cabinet-level champion for international human rights. During the tenure of the previous government, there was a Minister of State responsible for the Americas. I do not dispute the importance of engagement in the Americas, but Canada's voice on behalf of international human rights, in South Asia and the Middle East in particular, is necessarily unique, is uniquely powerful, and is needed. The creation of a Minister of State responsible for International Human Rights, perhaps combined with other functions, would help ensure that human rights issues are always included in the conversation (including human rights issues in the Americas). Notably, this would not be sufficient without the proper commitment from the individual appointed and from other Ministers. We've had too much empty name-changing and window dressing already. But, as a substantive step, this could make a real difference.

These policy proposals are pragmatic and respond to the challenges we face. Above that, they reflect Canadian values. We believe in the basic dignity and rights of all people. We must stand for that on the world stage. Those who believe that must continue to make the case: Canada can and should stand for something. It should stand for what we collectively believe is right.

Manufactured by Amazon.ca
Bolton, ON

20306169R00072